To: Jayne,

Be well + happy.

Thank You,

Sofia Mc Nellis

IT'S TIME TO REMEMBER

My Memories Journey and Dreams

Sofia McNellis

iUniverse, Inc.
New York   Bloomington

It's Time to Remember
My Memories Journey and Dreams

Copyright © 2009 Sofia McNellis

iUniverse books may be ordered through booksellers or by contacting:

iUniverse
1663 Liberty Drive
Bloomington, IN 47403
www.iuniverse.com
1-800-Authors (1-800-288-4677)

ISBN: 978-0-595-52241-5 (pbk)
ISBN: 978-0-595-62296-2 (ebook)

Printed in the United States of America

iUniverse rev. date: 8/05/09

ABOUT THE AUTHOR

I was born and raised in Philadelphia, Pa. The essence of my life has been influenced and determined by my Italian roots, customs and traditions. Sixteen years of a Catholic education has taught me who I am and armed me with faith, integrity and a sense of right and wrong in order to remain committed to my spiritual choice and Italian heritage.

My working career included twenty years of service as a teacher in the Catholic School plus twelve years working as a System's Analyst at General Electric Company. After GE I worked as an administrative assistant for CPCU, Chilton Publishing Co. and Becket & Lee Bankruptcy Law firm.

My recent retirement in Malvern, Pa has enabled me to spend time with my husband, Bill to explore, observe and experience new things with older and hopefully wiser eyes. It gives me time to resume my second love to teach others the joy of cooking.

My respect and love for words have driven me to fulfill a self-promised milestone to share my experiences, record the stories and memories of my family and to capture my thoughts and opinions in writing a book. I want to take the time to revisit the past, view the present and glimpse the future.

I dedicate this book to my cousin, Josephine,
my husband Bill, and my friends, Jane and Josephine

S.McN.

I offer this script to my cousin Josephine Singel, my champion who believed in me and encouraged me to write these words.

I give thanks to my husband without whom I could not have persevered. He is always at my side offering love and understanding. He listened to me, read my writing at all hours without complaint, offering encouragement and support.

I want to sincerely thank Jane Kollmer for her continuous support without whose help I would not have been able to complete this milestone.

Thanks to Josephine Hand for her friendship and kind words.

CONTENTS

PROLOGUE

The stories in this chapter describe the beginning of my quest into the world of writing. Stories of growing up in an Italian family are reminders of who I am and how precious my beginning and roots are to me. Most of the stories are self-explanatory, but some require a little explanation of their origin and background. "The Legacy", "The Window Was Her Salvation" and "The Healer" were written in memory of my grandmother, Josephine Pagano, who was my confidant, advisor and friend. She offered me wise and sage advice, imparting knowledge and understanding based on her experiences throughout her lifetime.

"The Legacy" speaks of grandmom as a very strong and intuitive spiritual person. She lived in South Philadelphia with her son, James Pagano. He was never married as they say in the Italian vernacular. She had arthritis in her joints and was unable to stay on her feet for long periods of time and had difficulty walking. Her physical boundary did not stop her from doing her daily chores, but she was unable to go outdoors. Although she spoke broken English, she made her point. There was a window in front of the house that literally was her salvation. It was her primary source of communication with the outside world. This memory inspired the poem "The Window Was Her Salvation."

"The Healer" relates a story told to me by her neighbors and my mother, Brigida Carusi. Grandmom took her religion to heart and prayed continuously for the health and safety of her family. She had a particular set of prayers she called the *grazione*, (Italian for "thanks"). Midnight on, Christmas Eve was the only time she could reveal the pattern of the prayers and the secret behind them.

I was very blessed to have her share the *grazione* with me. I say it daily and think of her always. Years later I was saying the *grazione* and wondered about the origin of this ritual. This is the story as my mother told it to me.

Grandmom experimented with roots and herbs, concocting potions and teas to heal and protect her family from illness during the The Depression. She used them to help her family survive colds, stomachaches and other maladies, which helped keep her family in reasonably good health and defray the costs of medical expenses.

One time, a vendor driving a horse and wagon stopped by her house. He was very upset and begged Grandmom to look at his horse, which had staggered and collapsed onto the pavement. Grandmom went over to the horse applied herbal cold compresses to his head and recited the *grazione* over him. All at once, the horse stood up as though nothing happened. She told the owner to take the horse home and let him rest and he would be fine. News of the story spread throughout the neighborhood, and before long, people from near and far started requesting her help. She had a particular talent for taking away migraine headaches. Her talent and aid was passed on to many people and continued for several years.

All of a sudden, just out of nowhere, she said "no" and stopped her visits and services. My mother asked her why and what happened to cause this change in her. She factually and firmly stated, "It is God's work, not mine."

I have attempted to give a brief synopsis of the contents of my work with the hope that you, the reader, will take the journey with me, reminiscing with my past and offering me indulgence, understanding, experience and patience with this undertaking.

"The human heart refuses to believe in a universe without a purpose."
Immanuel Kant

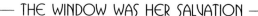 THE WINDOW WAS HER SALVATION

The window opens

Bright sunshine and light, fresh air tickling our nose and filling our lungs.
Cheery voices, friendly smiles, handshakes and waves, greetings from passers-by.
Shouts and screams from children and neighbors on the street, a sign of the grazione.[1]
Dogs barking, trucks and cars honking, wondrous sounds of God's talents and gifts.

Vendors deliver their goods tantalizing and fresh.
Friends seeking her wisdom, understanding and sage advice.
A momentary respite from the hustle and bustle.

The window closed:

Cloudy, stuffy, close, soundless and calm.

Sheltered behind the glass no salutations or voice from the usual traffic.
Muffled sounds of surrounding noises leaving one to imagine the origin and mystery hidden amongst the shadows, her eyes are closed in sleep — relaxed, resting at peace.

---

1   Grazione: a litany of prayers said repetitiously during times of worry and anxiety.

It is her time of solitude, meditation and prayer for family and friends asking for God's spiritual guidance, seeking courage and strength for life's journey.

A square geometric oasis amongst the bricks and mortar.
The Window at Grandmom's house.

A small street, a row home in South Philadelphia

Three bedrooms, kitchen, living room and bath

A family of six, mother, father, sister, brothers

A special person, matriarch, mother

Loving, caring, providing, comforting

Herbs, potions, lotions, concoctions, remedies

Massage, rub, stroke, manipulate

Hidden knowledge, inherited ability, a natural talent

Powerful hands, prayers and words sincere, in earnest, humble

Healing, releasing, helping

A special talent, her unique gift

Aches, pains, anxiety, removed, expunged, separated

Neighbors, family, friends relieved, set free, restored

Grateful, privileged, thankful, appreciative

Near and far, street to street, neighbor to neighbor

Seek, find, insist, demand, in need

Reflection of her gift and talent, realization dawned

It is God's work, His command, In His hands, His decision,

Out of her domain, a change in course, His job not hers

Stop, silence, termination, end

Position, status, title, new, energy redirected

Mother, grandmother, friend and confidant

Healer, a memory tucked in the past but not forgotten.

INTRODUCTION

I believe my ability to write is a gift God has given me in order to fulfill His plan for me. During the course of this experience I have questioned the how, why and when of this epiphany.

I never had inclination to write. My hobby and joy lie in cooking. So why is this drive to write possessing me now? It seems "turning 60" led me through some kind of metamorphosis. All of the sudden, I am more cognizant of my surroundings, people and things. I don't take things for granted. I feel the need to write and record my opinions and emotions. I am strongly motivated to leave a small testament of my existence here on earth. I want my niece and nephews to know their roots, take pride in their heritage and continue their Italian culture and traditions with their families.

I travel this journey trying to digest and absorb the signs along the way recording the experience. I was amazed to discover I had written over one hundred pages of text. I couldn't imagine that all those thoughts and words had come from me. Where do I go from here? What do I do with all of this? Questions were pouring from me, but no answers were forthcoming.

Out of the blue, my husband hands me an article he cut from the newspaper about a local English teacher who recently published his fourth book of poetry. It described his love of writing and how he decided to take a chance at publishing his work. Could this be an answer to my questions?

The following week, my best friend called to ask my permission to give my script to her neighbors who are retired publishers and whose son is a producer/screen writer for a popular TV soap for their review. She had been telling them about me to them and they said they would be interested in reading what I had written. My mood was positive and happy; I felt motivated to continue writing, and was anxious to hear what my reviewers had to say. Do I have any talent in this field? Was my writing worth pursuing? Several weeks passed and finally I received my answer.

To my shock and amazement, they were impressed with my writing and believed I have the ability to write and should begin immediately to coordinate all the pieces and format them into a book. They enjoyed reading the script and their words were "Go for it". God works in mysterious ways.

I never believed I had any talent or ability in this area of pursuit. I must confess I had no idea my writing was worthy of the compliments and praise I received. As a novice in this endeavor I am out of my element and seem to require instant feedback, motivation and sound advice to continue. The poems and stories were written as they came to mind. I would think of a title and the words would formulate and pour from my head onto the paper. I felt an overpowering desire to write these thoughts down. I wonder, is this how writers feel when creating their books?

I haven't a clue on how to write a book. I have been given several titles of helpful books to purchase to guide me and help in the start up process. I am not the kind of person who can read instructions and build a monument. I get bored easily and learn from hands-on try as I go methods, which are a huge frustration to my husband, as he is an engineer and has to read the directions several times, purchase the exact tools and methodically step by step put the object together slowly. My attention span and patience travel in the opposite directions. I just grab the nearest object and learn as I go. My destiny will determine whether I succeed or fail as I travel on this path but I am driven to give it a try, do the best I can and accept the outcome.

I want to break away from the routine, the norm and open my eyes to explore a new visionary journey. I want to have an open mind and heart to see, feel and experience people, places and things with a new perspective. I want to focus on the important things the core and guts of issues. I will ignore the nonsense and trivia seeing reality with clearer and older eyes thoughts and emotions.

I want to take a spiritual in-depth look at my life, rising above the trivial and identifying the real cause and effect of where destiny is leading me. I want to identify what is real and what is baggage to throw away the garbage and unimportant stuff concentrating on what is reality now. I have learned to use my faith and firsthand experiences to guide and help me to understand and see things with a new pair of eyes. I need to come out of the box set aside the old ideas and opinions and accept the new. I will think, act, react, express views, grasp and energize the power within to deal and handle whatever comes my way.

It is time to review my way of handling life's unexpected curveballs, trials and tribulations and the way I accept the good, bad, sorrowful and joyful realities of life. I will take time to explore life's mysteries, establish new boundaries, set new goals, and remove old habits to change my outlook. I will detour from the bad, take advantage of the good things and use them to learn, change and share ideas, thoughts and emotions. It is necessary to be open-minded and learn from others to be generous and giving without expecting something in return. I must finc-tune my attributes by setting an example with good qualities of honesty, integrity and morality.

I will take God's hand, hear, seek help, and embrace His gifts to strengthen my faith, hope and love. I must take them out of storage, they have been lying dormant too long and activate them to release my inner self. I need to put aside fear and anxiety speak out, set new goals establish new trends and face things head on. I promise to cherish and appreciate my friends and the time spent with family to be aware of my vulnerability and mortality. I wish to leave behind a legacy, of stories and memories, to record them for future generations to be remembered, entertained and enjoyed over and over in time.

We must all wake up, The time is now. We need to grab life by the tail and embrace it; learn from our mistakes; and savor all that is around us. We must stay alert, watch, listen, and learn to remain active keep in tune and stay in sync with current events, world news etc. Keep an open mind to new thoughts, things and ideas. Remember the past, embrace the present and experience the future.

Come share my journey, enjoy my poems and stories, identify and commiserate with my experiences and share my thoughts, joys and sorrows. Spiritually, prayer is our best weapon. God is always there to help us. He has given us the gift of inner strength, courage and fortitude. We have family and friends to anchor us and encourage and strengthen us during the difficult times.

I encourage you to follow your heart and travel the journey. I want to spark your engine to take the plunge, to be your own best friend.

The bible tells us that God created us with wisdom, free will and understanding without a price we must share and give without a price.

We need to freely apologize for our wrongs and practice humility, understanding and compassion. The rewards, gifts and emotional high gained is beyond anything imaginable. Life is too short, We must take inventory set the books straight and rethink our priorities, motivations, career and goals. Analyze and improve where we are and set a course for where we are going. We must give it our best effort because we have much to gain and little to loose. My visionary quest is to express my thoughts and visions and with pen and paper capture in writing my thoughts and experiences. Hopefully I will publish them fulfilling my lifetime dream on this literary journey.

"The mind comes before the voice."

CHAPTER 1

Being Your Own Person

Be your own person think before we speak. Unkind thoughtless words are impossible to recant.

I was raised by very strict parents in a traditional Italian family. My whereabouts and actions were monitored with a low tolerance for error.

On my twenty-fifth birthday, I felt it was time for me to liberate myself from my parent's house and venture into my very own apartment. I was scared witless but the feeling of freedom was well worth the pain. I met new friends, learned to budget my money and how to be comfortable in my own company. I enjoyed my time alone reading, cooking and listening to music, but I was missing one tiny little thing: the company of a man. In order to rectify this omission, my girlfriend Joanne introduced me to her Uncle Harold, who although a little older than me was also a fellow school teacher. We hit it off immediately and became very close and dear friends. Whenever we needed the so, called date, we would accompany one another to that particular occasion. He was a true companion and an interesting person to be with.

Eventually I met Sam, a police officer and we started to date. I invited him to my brother's wedding and he met the members of my family. Little did I know, but this innocent gesture would cause me pain. My aunts and uncles are rooted in their Italian beliefs and traditions and by their standards, they assumed that Sam was my soon- to- be husband.

My cousin was getting married and gave me the honor of being in her wedding party. In the Italian family, a large engagement party is given in order for all families to meet, to visit and become acquainted with each other. Whenever my aunt has a party, there is a roasted pig as the guest of honor. It is a unique experience to witness and enjoy depending on how you feel about eating meat from a whole pig. The butcher arrives donned with a white (alright, not so white) apron and cap; he delivers the whole pig (yes with an apple in its mouth) on a large wooden plank. He begins the ceremony by drinking homemade wine and singing Italian songs as he tosses his carving knives into the air and proceeds to carve the pig. The meat is very tender and spicy the skin crispy and delicious better than potato chips.

During a dinner with Harold, I mentioned the party and told him the story of the pig tradition. He was excited and wanted to see it firsthand, happily, I extended him an invitation to the party. While we were eating, I noticed my aunts and their friends staring at us and whispering to one another. I decided I was just overreacting and forgot about it.

Two weeks later, I received a call from my mother she said "your aunt called." She wanted to know who Harold was and where the police officer was? I explained that he had to work and Harold wanted to see the pig.

My mom told me "Your aunt doesn't want you to be in the wedding because you are not a good woman. I was not surprised, about the way my family thinks. I immediately called my cousin and explained the situation. Of course, she insisted I stay in the wedding. About one week before the wedding, I met the Italian priest who was going to say the Mass and perform the ceremony. He singled me out and told me he would not give me the sacrament of Communion because I was "not a good woman." I explained to him that it would destroy the joy of the day, but if that was his choice then I would not back down that I would walk up to the altar and receive Communion. Anyway fortunately my cousin and her fiance stepped in and diffused the situation. The wedding was beautiful and uneventful, except at the reception. One of the groom's uncles asked me to dance. Immediately his wife rushed over and brought him back to their table. I was a tainted woman and not to be trusted with any man.

Everything is not always as it appears on the surface. There may be a hidden agenda that triggers a negative response. My aunts were raised believing in certain rules and traditions that remained ingrained in their mind, which dictated their behavior. This event taught me that people will treat you the way you allow them to treat you. If I demand respect, I will receive it.

We are entitled to our own opinions, views and actions. We should not carry an obligation to agree with eveyone or offer rehearsed, canned answers repeating what people expect in order to remain on their good side. Telling the truth is uncomfortable and bears a high level of risk that carries consequences. We must establish parameters knowing when to draw the line and when to remain neutral and silent. We must be diplomatic, kind and considerate of the feelings and opinions of others without compromising our own beliefs.

There have been other occasions, for example at my father's funeral, where I was to hear those words "you are a bad woman" repeated once again. Since my mother would be alone in the house, it was assumed I would give up my apartment and move in with her. We discussed the idea, but she preferred to be alone to have peace and tranquility for a while. I often remember those words and I use them to take inventory of myself and review my goals, integrity and the moral codes, which I have designed and chosen for myself.

My aunts and I put aside our differences and shared our views and love through the good and bad times. We never held a grudge. We remained loyal and steadfast to one another. Family cannot be erased or expunged from our minds and hearts regardless of any rift, distance or misunderstanding because *La Familia e' dura e' forte*. The family is strong and everlasting.

I have come to realize that words impart power, strength and determination, testing our decisions and responses in times of crisis, tragedy, celebration, meditation and strife. They offer security, respite and calm, often being the only consolation I can offer during hard times.

WORDS

Words are the tools used to communicate one's feelings, desires, emotions and expressions.

They can be complimentary, loving, friendly and happy, creating a sense of good will and an upbeat attitude, motivating the recipient to achieve and succeed in whatever aspirations one sets his or her mind upon.

Words impart power, strength and determination, testing our decisions and responses in good times and bad times.

Words can be cruel, hurtful and evil, striking without warning, causing heartache, self-recrimination, low self-esteem and sadness, sending damaging blows both physical and psychological to its victims.

They have two forms – verbal and written. Which one is more effective? It depends on how the recipient perceives their meaning, the messages they are sending.

Reading a good book is very entertaining and allows the reader to escape into another world filled with fantasy, adventure and history.

Studying for a test, although tedious, will allow the reader to reap the rewards of their perseverance and persistence.

Praying in a peaceful calm environment allows one to express their innermost thoughts and feelings to a higher being, their God.

Listening to a lecture, TV show, prayer service can set the thought process into motion absorbing the message and knowledge designed to reach the listener.

Screaming obscenities or insults in times of stress, confusion and rage often in an uncontrolled environment will set into motion harmful damaging events beyond one's limit of control.

Words are the primary source of communication in our lives infusing knowledge and power within our thoughts. Man need not be afraid of the weapons/guns but terrified of your words.

We need to understand their importance. They give us the ability of expression, and the skill of oral verbiage. They demand our respect and appreciation for their role in the communication and expression governing our very existence.

We must be mindful of their effects and think before we speak using them to voice our opinions, impart knowledge, advice and understanding, praising and bringing joy to our fellowman.

Damnation or salvation, your choice!

SECRETS

Leaves the mouth,

once voiced it floats through the air.

Deep and intense, happy or sad picking up speed

traveling through space

place to place, destination unknown.

Exhausted it lands, settles and dies

to be replaced by a new one.

The cycle begins again!

MISTAKES

What circumstances, situations, conditions or events determine incorrect ideas, opinions and actions? Are there degrees or categories that measure the level of complexity prompting the occurrence of a mistake? How often does the mistake occur or for instance, become noticed?

Handy guides to preventing a faux pas, oops or embarrassment are experience, trial and error specifically, intuition helping us to assess the situation, read mood and attitude sensing the tone and feel of the event.

Mistakes can be humorous providing laughter and fun for example, watching the antics of babies, animals, sports, etc. The oops mistakes suggest something forgotten or an uncontrolled body function, an innuendo slightly embarrassing but of no consequence.

Mistakes, unfair judgement, gossip or misinformation are in a category singly defined. Mistake is an inappropriate term for such an error. This type of blunder offers severe consequences and repercussions and must be prevented at all costs.

Who determines the mistake, its type, level of severity and consequence? Is it the recipient? The perpetrator surely is cognizant of their actions and its effects. Embarrassment and blushing followed by an apology carry regret and consequence.

What are the qualifications and credentials required to enable someone to determine and pass judgement on the perpetrator of a mistake? As the recipient of verbal judgement and correction, they have a right to react and voice their comments whether negative or positive. Mishaps, oops, funny mistakes are harmless carrying a low level of consequence. Once the words have left the mouth, they cannot be retrieved; and impel severe, harmful mistakes carry long lasting effects which cannot be excused without sincere effort, retribution, correction and remorse.

It is our responsibility to make a conscious decision to prevent harmful errors in judgement and promote charitable behavior from others. I am reminded of the old saying, "What goes around comes around."

SORRY

Throughout our lifetime whether or not by default, intention, accident or circumstance, someone has experienced as a result of our actions, embarrassment, ill will, insult, displeasure or worse.

"I am sorry"; "It was my fault"; "Forgive me"; and "I apologize" are words seldom voiced, difficult to admit, complicated and strained demanding absolution and compassion.

Assuming responsibility for our transgressions, transcends many levels of sincerity and conviction requiring strength and courage exposing the composition and form of our personality. Facing conflicts, admitting blame and accepting fault are attributes learned as a result of education, religion, experience and the example of others.

How, when and what we do is determined by our upbringing, belief, morality and integrity. Believing and practicing what is preached, correcting the wrong, offering remorse and regret creates a sense of relief, good karma, peace and friendship. Right or wrong our intentions are spoken with honesty and sincerity. We have taken the first step, offering culpability and resolution while requesting understanding for our wrongdoing.

Realizing the error, accepting the ramifications and learning by our mistake, we promise never to repeat the offense although there is no guarantee of a congenial outcome. We have listened to our conscience and followed our heart in the hope of setting right a wrong what has been done to another.

CRITICISM

Helpful suggestions, casual comments, spontaneous words, unkind remarks

Spoken directly, off the cuff, or out of context

In jest, straightforward or to the point, direct or indirect

Whatever the case, reason, cause or prompt

Intellectual, work, projects, dining, exercising, conversation or activities

Helpful, kind, mean, gentle, thoughtful, harsh or hurtful

Sent, delivered, explained, written or verbal with minimal remorse

Criticize, punish, persuade, embarrass, belittle its intent the same

Correct, change, disassemble, fix, or discontinue

Loud, screaming, shouting sent, delivered, rendered

Wanted, unwanted, accepted or denied, yes or no

Taken in stride, get use to it, be a man, roll with the punches

Feelings/motivation dampened, crushed, encouraged, energized

Emotions stirred happy or sad, proud or disappointed

One of those things, part of the routine, an everyday occurrence

In jest, conversation, behind the back, second hand

Used, abused, disregarded or thrown away

Serious, unpleasant, circumstances good or bad

Better or worse, here to stay, existing, annoying, not going away

Take it or leave it, handle or not, swallow or spit it out

Criticism it's name and part of the game!

A Grudge

"Lord You forgive me, but can You make sure the other person does too?"

Questions: What is the length of time one holds an indiscretion against another?
Are there any guidelines or parameters set for such a situation?
Do the consequences or severity of the act determine time?
Are emotional reactions and personalities key players in equating the time factor?

The dilemma: Each of us has faced this dilemma either as the perpetrator or the recipient experiencing the same results regardless of status.

More often than not, the family or workplace is the prime environment for arguments and dissension, usually one word leading to a litany of them.

Little things trigger differences of opinions with heated debates escalating into tension and anger.

If not kept in check or immediately diffused, the situation creates an unpleasant scene and mushrooms out of control hissing and spitting loud angry threats, name-calling and malice leaving everyone present embarrassed and uncomfortable.

After both parties have vented their spleen, the aftermath leaves consequences of gossip, speculation, ill will and bad feelings all around.

Group or family gatherings for holidays, special events are affected creating an awkward position in planning, writing and sending the invitations becoming awkward and tedious rather than a fun activity. Will emotions be high, sides drawn? Who will attend? The host is unsure of the number of attendees, and which way mood, temperament and attitude of the guests will flow.

The disagreeing parties are petitioned by family members or co-workers to revisit the event with a calm perspective and a different attitude in analyzing their cause and effect. They are asked to reconsider their decision to offer an apology and create a peaceful truce that would result in a harmonious co-existence for all involved.

This result is ideal but unfortunately not always feasible, because the event has left invisible scars too damaging and hurtful to forget. One of the best options is if both parties agree to disagree especially in their place of work.

Another, a worse possible scenario, is for the afflicted parties to avoid further contact with one another thereby separating themselves from the possibility or repetition of an explosive situation. Whatever the option, it is time for differences to be settled, anger put aside, and life to move on.

"Life is merely changed, not ended,
that those I love are still with me though unseen."

A prayer to St. Anthony of Padua, Benedictine Abby, NY.

CHAPTER 2

Respect, Sacrifice, and Self Denial

When I am sad at the death of those who were close to me, may my sadness be firmly supported by my faith.

In the spring of 1985 my father, my best friend and confidant passed away. His passing was very devastating and a catalyst for major changes in the way I envisioned my life.

My father came to this land of opportunity to better himself, marry and raise a family. He was proud to be an American and believed that if you lived in this country, you participated and respected both Italian and American cultures.

He was a cement construction worker and labored long hours outdoors in all types of weather to make a living for our family. He taught himself to speak and read the English language and kept current with world events. He was very proud to have been born in this country and grateful for what he had.

My mother made sure we respected and honored him as the provider for our family. No matter what time he came home from work, she made us wait for him to have dinner. We respected his position as head of the family and always waited for him to fix his plate first. Then we would follow, with my mother being last.

My dad was very philosophical and had a saying for everything. His parenting methods were very unique. Dinner time was his chosen hour of the day to review the good and bad events of the day. When we did something bad, he would offer comment but delayed distributing the consequence. He would let us stew and worry as to when we would pay the piper. I will never forget the time my brother came home late and smelled of cigarette smoke. The next night while we were eating dinner discussing mundane topics my dad turned to my brother and said, "Son, you are like a pear on a tree. It hangs on the tree getting ripe until one day it falls from the tree". My brother knew later rather than sooner what that meant and how he would "pay the piper."

Two weeks later at dinner, we were discussing the day's events when my father took a plate and bopped my brother on the head. He said, "Son, the pear fell from the tree."

My father and I used to sit for hours discussing school, dating and all the important things I needed to understand in life. He and my mom would roll up the living room rug and teach me how to dance while singing Italian songs in my ear. As the boy in the family my brother was hanging out with his friends while I, on the other hand, had to remain home because I was the girl.

As I look back, I smile and can understand the self denial and unselfish sacrifices my parents made to provide a loving and caring home for us. The winters were hard on my family because the weather was too harsh for the workers to work outdoors. My dad used to shop at a warehouse buying non-perishable items to store away during hard times. Christmas was exceptionally hard as my parents could not afford presents. They would put up a tree and provide a wonderful Italian meal that began with the holiday soup and ended with fruit and nuts but there was not enough money for anything else. I will never forget the time my brother wanted a brand new bicycle. I was sixteen years old working after school at a photography studio helping out in the dark room and baby sitting the owner's children. I managed to save one hundred dollars for a new stereo record player. One day, I found my father sitting alone in his favorite chair with his head in his hands. Alarmed, I asked him what was the matter. He told me he was embarrassed and upset to think he could not get his son the bike he so badly wanted. I was very touched to see this side of my dad. I didn't realize he had such a tender heart. I offered to give him my money to buy the bike. He was lost for words and told me I was a good daughter. I can't describe my feelings to hear those words and to go with him to buy the bike. On Christmas morning my brother came down the steps and was totally speechless. His eyes were big as saucers and he started to jump up and down in pure delight. I thought he was going to wet his pants.

Dad went back to work in the spring and things started to return to normal. No matter how tight money was, my mom and dad always provided for us. Every Easter, they would buy us new Easter outfits with Dad's first paycheck. We believed that Easter was a time for a new beginning to wash away the old and start fresh. My Aunt Elisa worked in a chocolate factory and would bring home the seconds for us to eat. One year, she made us each a two-foot tall bunny rabbit made out of chocolate. It was too pretty to eat but we made the sacrifice. Now she is in her eighties and still worries and fusses over us. She is a very caring, loving and kind person and we are proud to call her our aunt.

We were raised to know right from wrong and to honor and respect one another and our family. In the Italian heritage, family is the core and essence of our being. Their lifestyle and example earned them our honor and respect and taught us to admit our faults and to right our wrongs no matter the consequence. That is what makes us who we are.

Armed with their teachings and philosophy along with God's gifts, we set out on our journey with a changed attitude. We are rejuvenated, energized and spiritually ready to follow the road, meet the challenges. We are armed with faith, hope and most of all love for family and for God. Spiritually, it is an opportunity for restitution, sacrifice, penance and change.

Dad

Dad, father, pop, daddy, sir

A title genetically linked, physically connected, flesh and blood

A name earned and respected

He is a part of our heritage, generation to generation.

Father to son/daughter, grandfather to grandson, infinite

An everlasting bond never broken, iron clad, firm and strong

Yelled, shouted and screamed during times of need, want, anger and exasperation

Beseeching, summoning, begging or cajoling we summon him.

Father, husband, companion untiring eternal love shared and passed on

Mr. Fix it, jack-of-all-trades, craftsman, bread winner, hard worker, the list is endless

A wise man, loving parent, shoulder to cry on, a steady hand, a caring heart

His knowledge, strength, experience, discipline firm and sure

His teaching and advice simple, honest and right

Taking nothing for granted, working hard in intense heat, bitter cold and inclement weather, he rarely missed a day of work.

Totally dedicated to his job, his responsibilities of home and hearth he provided the necessities for living comfortable, warm and protected.

Known for his sayings, philosophical, meaningful, applicable and true

His integrity unshakeable, honest to a fault, fairness and justice his creed

Although an immigrant he was proud to be in America, an American by birth.

Read newspapers, listened to the news remaining current with the times

Never wavering, constant, attentive, a loyal participant instinctively offering help and kindness to family and friends.

A daughter's love given unconditionally, permanent, sincere, enduring, steadfast

Privileged and proud to call him my dad, sharing trials and tribulations

Words non-existent insufficient in describing my loss, the pain in the heart, the ache in my soul

Sadly missed, forever remembered in pictures, memories, stories and dreams

Quietly voiced in a hush and a whisper, "I lost you dad, I miss you terribly.

Rest in peace in your new home, be with God, my prayers an offering.

Goodbye for now, I love you Nicolo Carusi, my confidant, companion, my dad."

THE GIFT

Small, medium, large, big or small

Whatever variety, size and shape

Fragile, bulky, heavy or light

Mailed, sent, carried or given

Boxed, bagged, loose, wrapped or unwrapped

Bows, ribbons, string or rope

Low budget, inexpensive or cheap

Costly, over the top, luxurious, break the bank

Wanted, appreciated, unexpected, needed, frivolous

Unwanted, off the wall, junk, useless item

Obliged, no choice, harassed, forced

Secret, intimate, private, precious, low key

Surprise, shock, unexpected, overwhelming, wonderful

From the heart, desire, enjoyment, willing

Holiday, weddings, birthdays, special occasions

Happy times, events, gatherings, parties

Peak, open, tear, rip apart

Whatever rhymes, reasons or cause

Appreciation shown, gratitude expressed

Shared together a cherished keepsake

The gift.

DEATH

End to life, termination, final departure

Expected, denied, for the best, accepted

Shock, numbness, hysteria, just a dream, disbelief

Quiet or loud, outward or inward

Overwhelming sadness, remorse and despair

Crying, moaning, rocking, trembling, expression/methods of comfort

Reflexes, feelings, tolerance, responses challenged

Strength and courage tested

Humanity explores ways to soothe the soul, calm a broken heart

Gone, not forgotten

Memories and stories a legacy left behind

Recanted and shared generation to generation

Advised, influenced, nagged, scolded, caring all given in love

Their image imprinted in our minds always and forever, infinite

Destiny fulfilled, a soul called home, a leap of faith

End of a journey reached, the final resting place, a spiritual reward

A new life, eternal, joyous and happy

Free of body, pure of heart, humble, vulnerable

Soul and spirit cleansed of sins, immortal, innocent, clean and clear

God's life companion

Death described.

PREPARATION

Dear Holy Spirit,

Dig deep into my soul and unearth the darkness.

Turnover the past its transgressions, sins and misdeeds.

I lay them before you, cleanse my soul and remove my guilt.

Show me the way to a new beginning in preparation for the Holy season of Advent.

I will follow the light so that I can lay a gift before my Savior on the Holy Day of His Birth.

Amen

REPARATION

How often have we taken time to unearth our dark side searching deep within our soul exposing it to the light laying it open for examination, remorse and contrition?

The seasons of Advent and Easter are times set aside to prepare and renew our faith to offer a commitment to the commandments, to firmly strengthen our belief in the teachings of the Church and renew our dedication to follow in God's Path.

It is a new beginning a renewal of Baptismal vows a time for contrition and forgiveness. In reviewing our past, we ask the Holy Spirit to fill us with new energy make us strong, courageous and to wipe the slate clean to begin again. We petition the Holy Spirit to fill us with His divine gifts energizing our body and soul to take action, set goals and determine our purpose to follow the word of God. Our prayers, actions and Communion are offered as gifts to Him in thanks for all the blessings and miracles He has bestowed on us.

As we reflect on the importance and significance of these special times in the Church, we are reminded of how He gave His life for our rebirth. How He suffered atrocities beyond our human comprehension to teach us and show us the way. His teachings whisper to our conscience of our duty and obligation toward our brothers and sisters in Christ promising to improve and right the wrongs we may have committed.

Rebirth, spiritual renewal, restored energy, new hope, strength, and purpose all of these rejuvenating us pushing us toward the light of resurrection and redemption. Praise and thanks to our Creator for His job well done.

THE WAY OF THE CROSS

Betrayal

Twelve people who hold your loyalty, love and trust with which you share your innermost secrets are gathered together seated at your dinner table. Which one of the twelve will it be? Who is the person that sends the arrow that pierces your heart? What is the catalyst that triggers such betrayal?

All of us carry within us the capability of such an act. With conscience or conscienceless during our lifetime, we have been guilty of inflicting hurt and sorrow toward someone we hold close.

Estate settlement, greed, divorce, jealousy and arrogance, mortal sins destroying families, squandering away a legacy, causing despair, hurt and sorrow; irrational behavior with the potential to lose something very special and dear to us.

Twelve apostles seated at the table sharing a meal with Christ. Judas silently counting his thirty pieces of silver uncomfortable squirming, plotting and scheming ready to carry out the deed and fulfill the prophecy. The plot is set, the participants in motion, the arrow is in place, aimed and ready to strike the heart of Christ.

Agony

In the Garden of Gethsemane, the apostles have fallen asleep leaving Christ alone with his thoughts in agony imaging the torture, pain and suffering that was to come. He calls out, "Father, if it is possible, take this from me". The silence surrounds Him as He faces the inevitable, raises His eyes upward and speaks, "Thy will be done".

Surgery, cancer treatments, mental illness, all diseases causing unbearable agony holding its victims in untold pain. In desperation they call out begging their God for relief from their suffering. "Lord take this from me." "Give me the courage, strength and peace to accept your will."

They are God's chosen ones. We have the privilege of sharing their faith, hope and love as we learn from their strength and courage to endure hardships and pain. They have shown that our complaints and troubles are small compared to theirs, reminding us of how fortunate and blessed we are.

Denial

Prophecy predicted that before the cock crows, Peter will deny the Lord three times.

Gossip, lies, falsehoods, derogatory remarks and indifference lie dormant within us activated by cowardice and anger set into motion ready to strike at any time. These forms of ammunition fueled the participants at the trial of Christ.

Just as the crowds lost their faith and hope, Peter was denying his association and connection with Christ. They stood before Pilot, their denial cowardice and anger predestined, unstoppable out of control propelling their screams mounting in crescendo, "Crucify Him", "Crucify Him" stabbing and piercing the heart of the Savior.

How often do we sit back and deny the atrocities and injustice around us? Our screams and protests kept silent because we are unwilling to break away from the crowd? Whenever we conjure up the courage to speak out, our voices are few and fall upon deaf ears.

Cross

Drugs, aberration, murder, rape, assault, each one a reed woven into the crown of thorns causing weakness, pain, bloodshed, and malice. The greatest evils that ever took place leading sinners into a dark dismissal place where the only way out is the greatest good, redemption. The longest journey taken one step at a time, the weight of the cross getting heavier and heavier, the distance overwhelming; all must reach the mountain and seek forgiveness. Whichever form of suffering whether emotional or spiritual, the way of the Cross will bring salvation. They must see themselves on the Cross, feel the darkness and pain, understand they are lost, work through their identity crisis and ask where they are going. They must focus on the image of Jesus and heal their wounds and take themselves off the cross. They must call out for help asking Christ to lighten the load to walk beside them just as Simon helped Jesus carry His Cross.

Crucifixion

How often has our capacity for suffering been tested? How many times have we called out those same words Christ called to His Father, "My God, My God, why have you forsaken Me?"

Christ suffered and died for us on the Cross in order to give us hope, take us out of the darkness of sin and bring us salvation. His humanity taught us everything is possible with Him. His sacrifice showed us the way to the light of faith and love. The prophecy must not go untold; we must spread the good news of Christ. Christ suffered the way of the cross giving His life for us. His example reminds us of our union with each other that all of us are brothers and sisters in Christ. As members of His team, we must remain committed to His mission. Imagine if we bring one soul home; what joy that would bring.

Home

Holy oil, a sacramental used in anointing the sick, Penance, Extreme Unction, restitution are the rituals and prayers of the last rites administered to the dying offering peace and forgiveness to follow the light and enter into the kingdom of Heaven. Christ rose from the dead in order to show us the way and bring us home. Lord, we thank you for showing us the way, the truth and the light. May the peace of the Lord be with us always.

THE CHRISTMAS TREE

Up down

Down Up, Up down

Straighten this, adjust that

Slide it back, pull it forward

Push it here, move it there

Open the branches wider, close them up

Standing in place tall and majestic

Waiting to be dressed, ornaments adorned and decorated

The angel tall and straight at the top guarding its domain

Lights twinkling shining bright

Rainbow colors reflecting off the TV screen and mirror

Multi-color old-fashioned balls dressing its branches

Ornaments old and new reminding us of memories passed, some yet to come

Go left, no right, one side then the other checking for stray wires, unwanted
gaps or flaws

Time for the garland a reminder of winter's frost
Turn on the switch
Ah! Perfect, perfect
Nostalgic, comforting and beautiful
The Christmas Tree

*"Memories created, stored away, tresures resurrected,
shared and savored for hard times."*

CHAPTER 3

REVERIE

We lived in West Philadelphia for seventeen years, where asphalt and cement was my playground. I would play stick ball in the street, ride my bike on the pavement and play ball and jacks on the stoop (front steps) with my friends. We were the only house with a breezeway, a large space between two row houses. My mother used to lay a large old bedspread on the concrete and make cookies and treats for us as we pretended we were in a park on a picnic. Our imaginations were filled with vivid pictures and images which allowed us to forget the gray and black to use our crayons to create and draw the colors of nature.

In the summer for four weeks, I would visit my grandmother and Uncle Jimmy. They showered me with so much love and affection, I thought I must be in a fairy tale. Grandmom had difficulty walking and her eyesight was failing, so I would go to the store and run her errands.

There was a mom and pop store that sold penny candy and an Italian bakery at the end of the block. After dinner, we would sit on the steps and smell the bread baking and I would go down and buy fresh baked rolls for all the neighbors. They would often give me pennies to spend in the candy store. There was a butcher/produce store that sold the best cream donuts in the world. I can still taste and feel that cream on my tongue. Even as an adult, Uncle Jim and grandmom would visit us every Sunday morning and bring us our favorite peppers and egg sandwiches and cream donuts.

I had three friends who lived in the same block as my grandmother and we became inseparable. We would walk to the soda/pizza shop and get a slice of pizza or a freshly baked soft pretzel and top it off with a double chocolate ice cream cone. The top of the cone had two openings for two scoops of ice cream with one handle on the bottom. Those tastes and smells would arouse our senses, leaving us salivating, invigorated and very happy.

My grandmom and uncle created a very warm and safe environment filled with love and affection. I was filled with peace and contentment knowing they would always be there for me.

My parents couldn't afford a shore vacation, but one year, a small miracle happened. My father helped a friend to build a cement patio in their yard. As a bonus for a job well done. The friend offered to let my dad use his house down the shore in Wildwood, NJ. We couldn't sleep for two days in anticipation of this wonderful adventure. Mom packed tons of food and Dad packed up his old jalopy for the trip.

It was a great adventure, the first time we would leave the city and go to see the ocean. We had no idea of the wonders we were about to experience. We had our faces glued to the windows of the car looking everywhere, enjoying the trees and flowers. As Dad was parking the car, we were disappointed to see that the house was on a street similar to the street we lived on in the city. My parents smiled and told us to be patient as they grabbed the beach paraphernalia took our hands and led us to paradise. We couldn't believe our eyes it was such a breathtaking sight. We felt the sand between our toes and the ocean breeze in our faces. We didn't know what to do or experience first.

Mom laid down a colorful blanket. With our bodies reclined and our eyes closed, we recorded the moment, trying to get relaxed and calm. The smell of the ocean filled our nostrils with stimulating fresh and clean air as we listened to the sound of the waves pounding the beach. We felt warm and cozy surrounded by the heat of the sun enfolding us within its warmth and comfort. It was a nice, pleasant and soothing experience that bonded us together as a family.

Our troubles were forgotten. We were thankful for the pleasures nature was offering us. Looking back on these memories of my childhood made me realize how important family is and the impact they had on my values and way of thinking. My parents taught me by their example. They lived their lives by working hard, being honest and sacrificing for the good of our family. They instilled in us their sense of high morals, love, affection, and respect attributes I will carry with me forever.

Every year my husband and I go to Cape May, NJ for one week. It is place where we take time to enjoy each other's company and recharge our batteries. Memories of a summer day long ago still embrace my soul and fill my heart with grateful affection, gratitude and joy for God's wonderful gift, my parents.

Peppers and Egg Sandwiches

Ingredients
4 green peppers
6 eggs
½ cup of grated cheese
Salt and pepper, to taste (if the cheese is salty, use less salt)

Method of Preparation
Cut green peppers into small strips and sauté in olive oil. Beat eggs with cheese, salt and pepper. Pour egg mixture over peppers and cook until it separates from the sides of the pan and is golden brown on the bottom. Take a plate and cover the pan and flip the omelette onto the plate. Slide the omelette back into the pan, allowing the other side to cook until cooked. Remove from the pan and cut into wedges and put into a fresh Italian roll.

Note: *This recipe is from Uncle Jim and grandmom. The secret is in how the peppers are cooked. They were just right, not mushy, but had a crispy texture. It is hard to describe and unfortunately, I can't remember how they were cooked.*

Cream Donuts

Around the corner from my grandmom's house, there was a small family-owned Italian grocery store called Ralphs. Uncle Jimmy would go there early in the morning and buy fresh rolls and especially the cream donuts. I have never found any donuts like the ones we had as kids. They were so fresh and filled to capacity with whipped cream. They tasted exceptional with a cold glass of milk.

AT THE BEACH

Sand, wind, surf

Seagulls, planes, adults, children

Beaches, water, lifeguards, tags

Umbrellas, chairs, mats, coolers, electronics

Buckets, boards, shovels, Frisbee

Sandcastles, collecting, water games, volleyball

Walking, basking, sleeping, floating, splashing, getting wet

Lotions, potions, tanning, burning, changing color

Time spent, happy, content, frivolous and gay

Sun going down, colors galore, beautiful

Until tomorrow, at the beach.

THE OCEAN

Back forth, in out, out in, forward, backward

Lapping, smacking, pounding surf

Fury, angry, calm, powerful, dangerous

Rough or smooth, murky or clear

Green, blue, brown, azure

Noisy, soothing, relaxing, hypnotic

Waves, ripples, undercurrent, riptides

Snowcaps, foam, frothy, curly

Cold, warm, hot, steamy, foggy

Deep fathom, sea life, caverns, caves

Coral, jellyfish, plankton, seaweed

Crabs, bivalves, whales, sharks, dolphins

Ships, boats, yacht, small craft, dingy

Divers, swimmers, lifeguards

Shells, stones, debris, pollution

Nature's wonder, the ocean!

BASKING IN THE SUN

Sunrays, tanning salon, heat lamp

Indoor or outdoor

Shore, mountains, lake, backyard

Sand, blanket, gravel, blacktop or grass

Oils, lotions, creams or spray

Sitting, standing whatever the position

Persistent perspiration, nature's antioxidant

Sweating, dripping fluids flowing, pouring down

Water essential, thirst quenched

Hot humid, sticky, clammy, burning

Faces, skin and bodies toasting turning color

Red, brown, bronze or beige, light or dark

Pallor gone, a picture of health

Fashionable, stylish and sleek

Suntan or sunburn the effect the same

Hot stuff!!

CRABS

Blue crustaceans

Shells hard, claws snapping

Sauce simmering

Water boiling

Pasta dancing

Crabs swimming, sucking in flavor.

Hammers banging

Picks picking

Meat escaping, dripping on chins, hands and elbows.

Lips smacking

Voices sounding

Mom's delicious crabs.

THE SUN

A ball of bright light golden shining in orbit
Its magnificence illuminating the sky
Awakening the Dawn rising us from slumber.

Rays of sunshine signifying eternal hope
Heating cold hearts and souls
Penetrating our bones soothing pain
A temporary respite from the bleakness
Cold and sorrow hidden in the clouds.

An array of color fantastic and awe
Inspiring challenging artists' palates
Our senses whirling, creating pictures
Of the beauty that surrounds us.

The phenomena of nature purging the sadness and melancholy from our
Thoughts, brightening our mood with happy plans and ideas
Infusing our souls by its warmth and splendor, lifting us higher and higher In
respect and appreciation thankful to its Creator.

Energizing our batteries, motivating our bodies to spring into activity
Exercising, running, limitless possibilities of the power within.

Wherever the place – beach, park, home, we cherish the day savoring Every
moment in time absorbing the light surrounding us
Happy and joyful in its embrace.

Light fades slowly descending through the clouds
A canvas of colors beyond our imagination silencing the noise
Its audience stunned and amazed, their eyes focused
Capturing every nuance, as it sets peaceful and calm.

Darkness surrounds us as spectators hushed
And in wonder walk away remembering.

Nature's gift, God's creation, the Sun.

Dining in Cape May

We recently returned from a vacation in Cape May, N.J. While eating dinner at a local Bed and Breakfast, we shared a delightful encounter. She stood tall, manicured and sophiscated. As she entered the room, an aura of mystery permeated the area. The waiter sat her at the table across from us. He greeted her with tender assistance and care. Her voice was clear and articulate, yet soft and pleasant to hear. Her countenance and demeanor caught our interest, sparking a need to satisfy our curiosity. I discretely questioned the waiter as to her identity. His eyes sparkled and his smile broadened as he said, "That is Miss Bessy."

She was eating dinner alone and seemed to know all the waiters by name. They were all fussing over her to ensure her comfort. Initially, we thought she was the owner or a relative of the owners. We learned through our waiter that she was 89 years old, and lo and behold, is an employee of the Bed & Breakfast. For the past 25 summers, she has made coffee and breakfast on the veranda for the guests every morning. She regales the guests with stories as she reminisces about the old style of life in Cape May. I hope to be like her at that age, so full of life, giving of herself with a caring heart.

FAVORS

A request, courtesy, boon, plea or good deed

Defined in the Thesaurus, their meaning the same

Back forth, back forth

Giver to recipient, recipient to giver

Give and take, sharing

These words ring true

Do me a favor and I'll do one for you!

THE HOUSE IN NEW JERSEY

For those who live in a busy metropolis, a second home is an oasis, a retreat from the routine of everyday activity.

It provides the owner with a sense of pride, an accomplishment for all the saving, hard work and sacrifice required to achieve this goal. It is a place for relaxation, fun, indulgence and sharing the company of friends and family.

Food plays a great part in the mix as it provides permission to partake of traditional and comforting foods, tasty calories otherwise forbidden in our daily diet.

It demands respect from the owner, provides an opportunity to dirty one's hands, nurture and feel the soil, be one with the land, grow produce for sharing. It offers an appreciation and an opportunity to gather and harvest its rewards and bountiful gifts, which are proudly displayed at the family table.

It is a meeting place for grand reunions, for bonding cousin with cousin, brother to sister, family with family. It is a haven for those who need their energy recharged, thoughts restored and cobwebs swept away from their thoughts. It is a place for creating and sharing memories to be stored away for reflection on a rainy day or to chase away the blues.

If you see someone standing on White Horse Pike in NJ waving you over, it is Uncle Rocky welcoming us promising recreation, good times and fun at his House in Berlin New Jersey.

CHAPTER 4

Acceptance and Hospitality

Imagine a leaf bag filled and tied with string. Loosen the string, we turn it upside down and watch the spilling of its contents of words, pictures and colors of the seasons onto the ground. We sort them, group them, visualize them, give them life, and use them to remember bad as well as good memories. We are driven to touch, feel and experience their euphoria, empowered by their meaning and intent. We remember times, past and present, savoring the moment and taking advantage of the changing of the seasons.

My memories take me back to my senior year of high school when we moved from Philadelphia to the suburbs in Havertown, Pa. Our new house had a small yard in the front and a larger one in the back of the house. It was a big step for us to leave the city and move up to the suburbs. We had no idea what it had to offer. Immediately upon arrival, my parents started to discuss the renovations and landscaping they planned to do in their new house. Mom planted trees, flowers and shrubbery in the front of the house while Dad planted a vegetable garden, including a peach and fig tree. You can't call yourself Italian if you don't have a fig tree.

Every summer, Mom would make fresh tomato gravy for pasta from the tomatoes and herbs grown in their garden. In the fall, she would help dad make homemade wine. They would cure the barrels and squeeze the grapes, producing a very pleasant and fruity wine. We would get together and help Dad rake the leaves. It was a real treat. Suddenly he went into the house and came out carrying an armful of potatoes. He wrapped them in foil and buried them into the embers of the burning leaves. After they were cooked, we put butter on them and ate them right outside with the butter dripping down over the rake and on to our sleeves.

Looking back on those times, I have grown to appreciate my Italian nationality and traditions. I must confess, I was embarrassed by the way we lived because the lifestyle of my friends and their parents was so contrary to mine. Our new neighbors kept their property beautifully manicured and landscaped. They wouldn't dream of planting vegetables or fruit trees. As a result they did not take kindly to my parents and frowned on their plans for the garden. They were condescending and mean in their thoughts and manner toward us. Sundays were the only day my dad was free and whenever he would hammer or use his tools to fix the house, they would complain. On one occasion, they called the police. The policeman was very kind and understanding to my father and advised him to work later in the day and explained the township rules to him.

However things have a way of turning around. Our neighbor's sidewalk was continuous with ours and both needed to be replaced. My father dug up the old and replaced both sidewalks free of charge to our neighbors. They were shocked and grateful for the gesture. It was difficult for them to acknowledge us but they befriended my family and we became friends. They came to accept us by who we were-not as a stereotype of someone else.

Little did I know that years later, I would experience the meaning and effects of prejudice. I was in my early twenties teaching in a Catholic School surrounded by religious nuns during the day and my strict parents at night. I was very naïve and innocent and self conscious about my weight. I had very few dates and read a lot of books. A male teacher was hired to observe at my school. He was nice looking, smart and also overweight. He was very outgoing and, to my amazement, asked me out on a date. Several dates later, when out of the blue he asked to meet my parents. I thought it was unusual but I agreed to bring him home for dinner. My parents were happy and my mother started to plan the meal and clean the house because an important guest was coming to dinner. The date was set during the week, as he lived in New York and traveled home on the weekends.

After working in the hot sun all day, my father would come home, shower and put on a tee shirt and clean work pants. He was always puttering around the house fixing things or tending the garden. Also it helped cool off his sunburned skin. When we arrived, my parents were sitting on the front porch, anxiously waiting our arrival. I introduced Robert to them and we sat down to chat. My mother left us to go prepare the meal and my father went to get his homemade wine. Robert pulled me aside and angrily preceded to inform me that he would not be staying for dinner. I was shocked and completely taken by surprise. He told me that my family was not of the right class, that it was disgusting to see my father wearing a tee shirt and my mother in a house dress. His father was the owner of a very popular high class magazine and he would be embarrassed and mortified to present us to his friends and family. His family entertained with garden parties and catered dinner that their servants and staff prepared. Words could not explain my feelings of embarrassment and hurt for my parents and myself. For a long time, I did not bring anyone home to see my house or meet my parents. In my innocence it didn't dawn on me that I was a victim of prejudice. Looking back on that incident I regret my reaction and the attitude I assumed. My age and experience have taught me to accept myself for who I am and to appreciate my Italian roots.

Our house was a happy place where family and friends dropped by often to chat and visit with us. No invitation was necessary. If you were in the neighborhood, the door was always open. It amazes me that whenever we gather together for festivities, we all revert to the favorite foods from our childhood, background and culture. The current buzzword is comfort foods, appropriately titled promising joy and satisfaction. My mother always had plenty of food on hand as she was an excellent cook, and Dad kept the wine flowing. Everyone would hate to leave because they felt at home, nourished and comforted.

On cold winter nights, our parents entertained us with stories and memories reminiscent of their past, family, trials, and tribulations in conjunction with the history of our ancestors. My father, keeping up our Italian heritage, told stories of his family life in Italy while my mother recanted tales of her American culture and traditions. Their thoughts and experiences have been handed down to us to be passed on, treasured, remembered and shared for those cold winter nights when history repeats itself.

The desire, love and passion for Italian cuisine have been handed down to me from generation to generation, grandparents to our parents, from me to my brother and him to his children. Nicholas, named after my father, has recently graduated from a well- known Culinary Institute in Atlanta. He is an executive chef and manager of a five star restaurant as well as a caterer and teacher. Michael is pursuing a career in chemistry and environmental technology, while Bridget has a special gift for writing and computer skills and works part-time at a restaurant while attending college.

Coincidentally, my grandmother on my mother's side was also skilled in making foods but on a different level. Her expertise was dedicated to the chemical development, reactions and proportions of foods. She made pastas of every shape by hand, pastries, desserts, canned vegetables and jarred pickles and eggplant, and bottled her own root beer and beer. She used herbs to make potions and remedies for their common aliments.

In comparison, each had talent for different aspects of cooking – one an expert in preparation, ingredients and artistic presentation, and the other a specialist with hands-on knowledge of the composition and natural elements of foods and their preservation. Regardless of the category, the food was abundant, delicious and mouth watering causing people to crave a taste.

These Italian immigrants were people of humble origin, without formal schooling and limited opportunity, who realized their potential, took a chance, made their own rules and stepped out into the unknown. In their time, this was unheard of and frowned upon, as the men were the kings of the hill. My grandmothers established themselves and set up a business utilizing their skills, wits and talent to better their lives, provide for their needs and secure a safe and comfortable environment for their children. Our forefathers'and grandmothers' independence, stamina, power and wisdom have left a memorable imprint, a marker of their legacy, of their memories and accomplishments to be honored with pride and dignity. They have motivated, influenced and empowered us, the future generations, by their virtues, enabling us to overcome obstacles, pursue our talents and dreams, and follow our heart.

We breathe in their scents, stimulate our senses and enjoy their magic, absorbing all the beauty their images and sounds provide. We allow and accept the changes to occur from within scattering them about and sharing them with others. We are motivated to create a story, discuss their origin, see the beauty, and become a visionary utilizing the gifts they offer.

God's special people, His gift, we give thanks as we follow in their footsteps. We are a work in progress, a legacy to be remembered and cherished.

Sunday Mornings

Aromas of simmering chicken soup, gravy, meatballs, sausage in the pan fill the air tingling our nostrils, stimulating our taste buds and teasing us into submission to leave our bed, mom's unique alarm clock.

Entering the kitchen, we see mom bent over the kitchen table making homemade macaroni to be married with gravy and freshly grated cheese paired along side of a large bowl of meat from the gravy.

Dad is in the city at an Italian deli purchasing fresh made cheese, bread and prosciutto for his specialty, the antipasto salad. Included in this excursion is a side trip to the Overbrook Italian/American Club, a legitimate excuse for hanging out with the boys.

Like clockwork, mom rises early every Sunday to prepare the family meal, which through force of habit, dictate her to serve at exactly/precisely 12 o'clock noon. Absence at the table is unacceptable, and no excuse except death is tolerated. Our dad as head of the house insists on eating at this time, and we respect his position in the hierarchy of command.

The meal begins with homemade everything. No store bought pre-made meals in our house, or for that matter, in any Italian household, as it is a sacrilege to even consider such an abomination. Mom prepares and cooks a variety of foods including chicken soup, gravy/meat, vegetables and a roast chicken, which are eaten fresh that day then heated as leftovers or taken for lunch during the week. Just imagine the menu for company and holidays. In consideration of the reader's weight and appetite, I won't go there.

Seated around the table we discuss a variety of topics and share stories of the old days, our thoughts and opinions while our taste buds are being overloaded by the delicious bounty. The last morsel consumed, we rise from our assigned chair only to collapse into another with stomachs fully sated and eyes drowsy with sleep from devouring such a feast. I read a book, my brother does homework, dad watches TV and mom cleans up and restores things to order.

Upon reflection, my mother never asked us to help her with the dishes and clean up. I guess she assumed that this was part of her job as a dedicated wife and mother and we were husband and kids prospectively each with our own place and responsibility. I wish I knew then what I realize and appreciate with all my heart now is how spoiled, lovingly cared for and lucky we are to have such a dedicated wonderful person in our life.

The kitchen shiny and sparkling, everything put away, mom joins us in the living room proud, satisfied and happy another meal completed. She relaxes in her chair planning her week and gathering her thoughts taking a well-deserved break, until the next time.

Like my mother, my brother and I strive to continue and uphold the legacy, heritage and traditions of two loving parents, dad deceased, mom now 87 thankfully alive and still kicking, so that future generations will know and understand from where they came.

Thank you mom for Sunday mornings, cherished memories.

SUNDAY GRAVY WITH MEATBALLS, SAUSAGE AND SPARERIBS

Ingredients
4 cans of plum tomatoes
1 15-oz. can of tomato sauce
8 cloves of garlic (if large cloves, use 5)
1/2 cup chopped Italian parsley
½ stick of pepperoni, skin removed
1 lb. Italian sausage (sweet or hot)
1 lb. of lean pork spare ribs
2 veal and 2 pork neck bones (optional)
1/2 cup fresh basil
1 large carrot

Method of Preparation
Pour tomatoes into a large pot and crush them with your hands. Add the garlic, parsley, carrot and half of the basil. Bring the pot to a simmer and simmer for 5 minutes and add the pepperoni. Meanwhile, prepare the meat for the meatballs and set aside (recipe follows); cut the sausage into small pieces. Rinse the bones and spareribs under cold water and season with salt, pepper and meat tenderizer. Line a cookie sheet with foil and place the spareribs and bones in the pan. Put into a 375-degree oven and let brown. On another cookie sheet lined with foil place the sausage, prick it and cook until brown. Take the cooked sausage out of the pan and place the uncooked meatballs in the pan. Cook them until they are brown.

Note: The following step is optional. Mom takes the pan with the foil from the meats and adds a little bit of gravy from the pot and patiently and carefully scrapes up the fond (bits and pieces) from the foil. Pour the gravy back into the gravy pot.

Add all the meats to the gravy and simmer it for 3 to 4 hours or until it thick. Separate the meat from the gravy and place the gravy into a food mill. Pour the milled gravy and the meat into the pot and simmer for another 10 minutes, adding the remaining half of fresh basil.

Note: As a matter of taste, if you prefer chunky gravy, skip the step with the food mill.

Meatballs

Ingredients
1 lb. ground beef
2 medium eggs (or 1 jumbo)
Salt and black pepper, to taste
¼ cup fresh chopped parsley
¼ cup grated Locatelli cheese
½ teaspoon garlic powder
½ cup Italian flavored bread crumbs (if mixture is too soft, add more bread crumbs)

Method of Preparation

Place meat into a bowl, add all the above ingredients. Mix together. Pick up meat with four fingers and roll into a firm ball. This is Mom's way to make them all the same size.

Place on a foil-lined cookie sheet sprayed with an olive oil spray and bake in a 375-degree oven. Remove when browned on all sides.

Note: *Mom made the meat mixture moist in order to avoid dry meatballs, especially since she didn't cook them in the gravy.*

Another option is to fry the meatballs in a little olive oil until brown. They are tastier this way. Browning them in the oven cooks them uniformly as frying them is hard to brown on all sides. If you have the patience, frying them is the true Italian recipe.

A great way to taste the gravy is to get a piece of Italian bread and spoon the gravy from the pot onto the bread. Sprinkle grated cheese on top of bread. Delicious! My brother and I would get up on a Sunday morning and eat this for breakfast.

THE VISIT

Gather the linens, sheets and towels
Make the beds, clean, straighten, freshen up
Move, shake, arrange, get ready
Go, go, go.

Check the pantry, buy the food
Plan the menu, shop for supplies
Cook, cook, cook.

In the car, on the way, busy long hours, many miles
Boring, tedious, eyes strained, body tense, nerves on edge
Traveling, driving, a trip long overdue
Hurry, hurry, hurry.

Unbelievable, dreaming, can't be true
Anticipation, excitement, anxious
Eyes peeking, feet pacing, ears listening
Waiting, waiting, waiting.

Car parks, horn honks, doors open
Luggage, bags, paraphernalia, stuff
Disembark, unpack, unload
Rush, rush, rush.

Hungry, thirsty, tired, discombobulated
Sleep, eat, hospitality provided, comfort stressed
Chill, chill, chill.

Settled, all together, gathered, grouped
Catching up, so much to say, each his turn
Talking, talking, talking.

Friends, family, invitations, parties
Here, there, everywhere
Going, going, going.

Ecstasy, delight, excitement
Brother, wife, niece and nephews
Safe, warm, bonding, united
Enjoy, enjoy, enjoy.

A favor granted, God's kindness
Thank You, thank You, thank You
The Visit

The Story

A country foreign, obscure, far away
Little villages tucked in the mountains
Simple folk, old fashioned, set in their ways
Quiet, peaceful, serene, unencumbered

Man:
Tall, lean, good-looking, above average, not handsome
House untidy, messy dusty, dirty dishes, clothes wrinkled strewn everywhere
A connoisseur, lover of food, home cooked, rustic, tantalizing, tasty and delicious
Consumed, obsessed, yearning, desiring, senses salivating in anticipation
Help needed immediate, critical, desperate
Seek, find, hunt, capture
Search, searching, searched, conquered
Victory, triumph, successful, lucky
Euphoria, excitement, jubilation, joy

Wife:
Rosy cheeks, tall, slim, well proportioned
Attractive, good-looking, a sight to behold, beautiful, pretty
Skills, proficiency, ability, handiness negligible, bad to worse
Every meal, burnt, greasy, uneatable, lousy, damaging to the palate

He:
Shock, disappointment, disgust, antipathy
Food, food, food, always on the brain
Appetite, desire, want spoken constantly, mind always centered on food

Mistakes tolerated, excused, forgiven, feelings consoled, soothed
Strive, endeavor, make an effort, try again, experience the teacher

She:
Too busy, no time for cooking, annoying, bothersome
Boring, no interest, indifferent, negative attitude, bad feelings
Firm, single minded, determined, resolute

He:
Ridiculous, inexcusable, intolerable, must change
Weak, hungry, stomach growling, empty
Anger building, frustrated, a volcano ready to erupt and explode

Situation out of control, impossible, unfeasible, not fixable
Decisions, decisions, decisions, think, choose, act
Food or wife, wife or food, an impossible decision, a difficult choice
Think, ponder, agonize, worry, what to do? what to do?
No alternative, remedy, option or solution

She:
Bullheaded, stern, unchangeable, stubborn

>   Stalemate situation stymied, stuck, deadlocked
>   Food, food, food, belly filling, hearty, satisfying
>   No competition, stomach first nothing else to do, decision final
>   Divorce, divorce, divorce, complete, done
>   "I can't eat beauty", farewell, so long, goodbye!
>   "Charm is deceptive beauty fleeting."

"Let us give thanks to the Lord; it is right and just."

THANKS

T   thoughts, talent, things, time, trust

H   health, help, hands, happiness, handsome, hope

A   ancestors, again, aunts, animals, answers, angels

N   nephews, niece, news, Neverland

K   kindness, kids, kindred, knights, king's pieces in chess

S   success, stuff, strength, silence, solitude, spirit

Thanks to You the Creator, God.

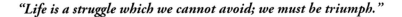

"Life is a struggle which we cannot avoid; we must be triumph."

CHAPTER 5

UNCONDITIONAL LOVE

The temperature is below freezing, and the trees are covered with snow. It is abnormally quiet, except for the blowing and howling of the wind rattling the trees and windows. Outside, the snow is swirling, covering the landscape with a blanket of white; inside, the fireplace is glowing, spreading a warm yellow light and calming my anxious thoughts offering heat and comfort.

Suddenly, I started to experience flashbacks into time. My mind kept wandering and finally settled on a memory back in December when my mother came to live with my husband and me. She helped design her own apartment in the basement of our house in Malvern, Pa. She was the oldest person living in the neighborhood. She maintained her independence, handled her finances and was able to plant a garden. She was very energetic and feisty, giving us sound advice from her seventy-five years of experience. For the first time in her life, she was totally independent and able to make her own decisions to live her life in her own way. She was truly happy and very liberated and at peace with herself.

Initially, it was pleasant and comfortable mother and daughter sharing and bonding, but as the saying goes, "all good things must come to an end." Time, age and physical deterioration have affected my mother's psyche, mobility and her degree of dependency.

Little did I know what the words "caregiver" entailed-the sheer stamina, courage, responsibility and guts required to fulfill this commitment toward an elderly person in this situation.

Although it was very difficult at times, I wanted to keep her with me as long as possible. I shared my energy with her to keep her alive and happy because I felt privileged to do it, but there are times I lost it. I can't conceive of life without her being with me and I constantly prayed for both of us to have the courage and strength to endure.

A caregiver sits, waits and watches her loved one's condition progress and deteriorate as each part of her body is breaking down, worn out and unable to function or control. Days, hours, minutes ticking away waiting and watching; watching and waiting one day superimposing the other undistinguishable constant indifferent of time or place unable to stop the clock from leading her to her final journey.

All options exhausted, she is at God's mercy. We implore Him to help us to endure the pain and suffering. Her time is in your hands, Lord; I fervently ask that you calm her and give her peace on this, her final journey.

She lived to be 89 years old a privileged and special time of sharing moments, thoughts, and joys creating memories to recall and reflect upon later on. Her death is a constant ache so deep with gut-wrenching sadness and endless tears that will forever be a part of me. They are so personal that they extend beyond the physical. It is a spiritual and mental loss unique to me, privately grieved within my heart and soul.

It is amazing to me how this whole experience reminds me of my own vulnerability on aging. I never thought about how I would age and what physical effects I will experience. Will I age gracefully or become dependent on someone? I do not have any children and promise that I will never place the burden of my care on any friend or family member. I am in the process of arranging my elder care so that I will have a plan in place for my senior years. Frankly, this whole scenario is more information than I want or need to know.

As I reminisce, I am captured by the flames in the fireplace. They mesmerize me, giving me a sense of peace and comfort. Their constant brightness reminds me of the good times I spent with my best friend, my mom.

I share these private and special thoughts with you so that they will be a comfort to those of you who have experienced the burden of these trying circumstances and events. I hope it will help you to realize that you are not alone in your sorrow and grief that I have gone through it and together with lots of prayers and with God's help we will endure and get through what life gives us.

Happy thoughts replace the sadness. They help chase away the winter blues sparking memories of the holidays spent with family and friends. The tastes and smells of food satisfy my senses; the atmosphere of love lingers touching that special place within my heart. The peace and contentment of this moment embraces and enfolds me within a spiritual blanket, offering contentment and relaxation within my soul.

Tomorrow's events will come regardless of time and place; but for now, all is cozy, warm and safe within this room.

UNCONDITIONAL LOVE

Its birthright requires a pure and loving heart,
Constant never ending, durable and strong.

Its rhythm beats to life's destiny a part of oneself.
True to itself never false, instinctively given natural, free and clear.

Its recipients selected from within
Its soul virtuous, confident and absolute.

Never restricted by time, space, purpose and cause,
It possesses no boundaries, qualifications, consequences or requirements.

It holds infinitesimal power at its command.
Reciprocation, gratitude, reward a non-issue in thought or expectation.

Regardless of circumstance, trouble, joy or strife,
Whatever the reason or condition, the commitment's the same.

Failure, mediocrity, refusal and denial conquered and slain never to rise.
Always ready to give not receive, explosive, forceful and strong extending
love and Understanding silently given from within, not loud or boisterous.

A love precious and rare given unconditionally always and everlasting.

THE LETTER

Dear Mom,

How do I list all the thoughts and expressions of you that formulate, tumble, and spin inside my head?

Where do I go to find a way to say them letting you hear them in ways not already used or heard?

What voice can I use to tell you of my heart, my very being that is bursting with the love, admiration and joy stored within me?

Listening to a recording, or reading the written word meager options too mild, weak lacking physical contact, feeling and power.

I realize that feelings, words and expressions must come from oneself told face to face, person-to-person yet I find it difficult and a bit uncomfortable to sit and bare my soul to you. These words are within me never silent pushing, shoving, compelling a conversation long overdue that must be heard.

In my haste I often loose patience become distant not by intention but by circumstance. Tolerate my faults, forgive my anger, harsh words and unconscious indifference, and forget my mistakes and unkind actions. Any wrongdoing, hurtful remarks I may have done to cause you pain or anxiety I am truly sorry and offer you my sincere apology. We must not forget that we are one, a family, and blood related, total for life, inseparable.

Mom, God has given you to me. I am a part of you soul-to-soul, spirit-to-spirit, heart to heart bonded together sharing and loving. Together we cry tears of sadness during death and hardship offer sounds of pride while laughing and smiling in times of happiness and joy.

Mom, this is the difficult part where I must remove the shield and say it plain and clear I love you with all my heart and soul. Thank you for my birth, childhood and adolescence those impossible trying times you had to endure teaching discipline, showing me the right of way. You made me an adult, the person I am today striving to follow your rules always to be truthful, never lie, be honest, make a good name for yourself and ask God to open that good door. Wisdom and memories cherished humble never to be forgotten.

In my maturity I have come to realize how right you are your eighty nine years of experience has guided you earned you the right to correct my errors, challenge my decisions and state your ideas, solutions and opinions. I am so blessed to have you with me and pray everyday for God to keep you with me, make you healthy keep you safe, warm and happy.

At a quiet moment and in a special place and time we will sit together you and I Daughter to Mother and we will have that belated conversation, I will read aloud this letter and fulfill a promise made from my heart a gift from me to you.

DECISIONS

Judgment, determination, choice.

Simple or difficult, light or heavy.

Weighing on the mind, testing our will, thought process and reasoning capability requiring undetermined amounts of time, resolve and patience.

Our courage and stamina strained, working, thinking, weighing, turning thoughts, options and possibilities over and over rationalizing all the issues, each consequence and repercussion. Some life alternating, possibly threatening, financially challenged affecting health and the future.

Advice and counsel from professionals, friends and family are reviewed, studied, pondered over; many times often helpful, factual, sometimes blunt forcing a check at reality. We take another look at the cause; review, revisit, and dissect it. Having been influenced, assisted, hindered or stymied, we painstakingly re-approach all the facts, options, recommendations, solutions and long-term possibilities with a different perspective, a confident attitude weighing the pros and cons in a new light.

Once formed, the wheels are set into motion, the page is turned, the responsibility, sole ownership, good or bad is final, irreversible, not turning back or erasing the page. Although exhausted, satisfaction and relief wash over us, apprehension and fear guarded, set aside, the process complete.

The mind is settled, set free. The decision determined in place; we move forward prepared, ready, standing tall, strong dealing with the outcome, the future.

Conscience

"If I can face the dark I can live the light."

Curtains drawn, lights out, the room is shrouded in darkness. Eyes closed I lay awake with my mind in thought and sleep a distance away.

The day's events are scattered all in a jumble for me to put in order. Questions and answers sorted and digested, all my activities and decisions in need of a final review.

Words and deeds constant and true, my guardian angel always at my side guiding my faith and background to dictate the right of way.

I examine my conscience with a verdict of not guilty, free and clear of wrongdoing and indiscretion toward my fellowman.

Restful and calm the night peaceful dreaming, smiling I fall asleep anticipating the rising of the sun, the dawning of a new day my conscience clear.

THE CALLING

How do we prepare our soul for the spiritual voyage into God's Kingdom?

The teachings and liturgies of our worship prepare and arm us with Faith, Hope and Charity, the cornerstones and tools of our belief.

Our actions, behavior, good works and deeds performed according to God's plan earn us the graces and indulgence needed for eternal salvation.

We ask the Lord to show us the way and lead us on the right path.

Our humanity and free will given to us by God through His Death and Resurrection are often influenced by worldly temptations. They are tempting us to detour off the right path, an everyday struggle that requires God's help and guidance.

The road is strewn with doubts and questions of disbelief and hypocrisy lacking love and spirituality challenging our faith at every turn.

Relationships with associates, family and friends test our emotional decisions, responses and reactions during the times of anger, trouble and strife.

Rosaries, masses, prayers and penance offered in faith cleanse our soul and prepare our mind and spirit to accept God's will as a member of our religious community.

Our faith tells us that if we live the good life and follow in His footsteps, His light will lead us to eternity.

The calling hails us. We feel its pulling forces motivating us to stay on track, follow our destiny. Our path is predetermined although our steps may falter stumbling, crawling or walking we continue to persevere down the path of rightness toward our final resting place.

We see the signs along the way: miracles big and small, prayers answered encouraging and motivating us to follow the beautiful light illuminating the road.

His words of strength, steadfastness, love and endearment keep us on course enabling us to fulfill our destiny, opening the doors to the afterlife. We respond to Your calling fearless and calm. "For You are the way, the truth and the light."

Faith

F irm statement of our beliefs and practices.
A ggressive resolve in defending the rights of others.
I nteraction with the rites of worship.
T ruth and integrity in oneself.
H aving the desire to fulfill the promise we aspire to.

Hope

H andling awkward situations with reasonable calm and understanding.
O peness to respect all Christians and non-Christians.
P rudence in decisions for others and ourselves.
E verlasting dedication and loyalty in times of uncertainty.

Charity

C hoosing to stay the course directed by conscience.
H elping our spiritual leaders in their vow of service.
A ctive service in lending a helping hand to the afflicted and unfortunate in our midst.
R easonable and just behavior when interacting with members of the faith community.
I nvolvement in the teachings, liturgy and activities of our religion of choice.
T rusting in ourselves to follow God's plan.
Y earning for God's graces and blessings guiding our free will to choose right from wrong.

Faith, Hope and Charity – the greatest of these is love and peace, the foundations of the universe; world's national security fighting aggression, evil, terrorism and justice, arming the faithful with keys to the kingdom of God.

Prayer

A single word, sentence or song

An entreaty, solemn request or thanksgiving

Holy, pious, profound, powerful

Honesty, sincerity, belief, glory

Act of faith, personal, conscience, private

Offered, sent, praised, petitioned

Helped, granted, sanctified, rescued

Hope, courage, wisdom, strength freely given

Quiet moments, troubled, times, hardship, sickness, death

Accepted, supportive, sustained

God's infinite grace

His blessings bestowed

Prayer

THE ROSARY

A string of beads chain linked, a cross its completion
Aesthetically textured rough or smooth
Blessed with holiness according to rule.
Beautiful yet simple functional and plain
Designed by Faith, Rosary the name.

Held within hands comfortable and sure
Voices resounding in dedication and praise.
Hail Mary, Our Father, Glory be,
Mysteries included, the mantra the same.

Whatever the time or place, situation or cause
God's blessings descending,
Overwhelming feelings of comfort, peace and joy
Lighting our spirits, strengthening our souls.

With graces earned, the noise silent, our petitions sent
We sign the cross, the ritual complete.

THE HEART

Don't make it sad or unhappy

Share your comfort, warmth and strength

Bring it peace, joy and hope.

It is precious, sensitive, forgiving, the central core of love within us.

Beating, ticking, constant, true, strong, steadfast

Life's caregiver

Offered unencumbered, without censure, malice or condition

Respect it, bond with it, love it, bring fulfillment.

Two hearts united, joined together in laughter, sadness, tears or smiles

Forever and ever.

Cherish, honor and care for it.

It is my heart I gift to you!

ANXIETY

A cruel painful, agonizing invasion of our psyche attacks our minds and thoughts leaving us vulnerable and weak. Fear, anticipation, nervousness and worry are all part of the process. It represses our abilities, haunts our thoughts and controls our decisions and plans. Regardless of the type – mild or severe – the ramifications are the same. The possibilities of harmful damage is staggering.

Anticipation of a sporting event, completion of a book can be at best annoying or exciting ending pleasantly or satisfactory.

Agonizing over medical results, financial investments, employment status, or life altering changes is more complex, out of our realm and beyond our control, because we are dependent on the expertise, knowledge and experience of others. We are subjected to the schedules and time constraints of others without input or suggestion.

This anxiety lies dormant within us simmering under the surface abiding time ready to strike without warning or pause unforgiving taking no prisoners. We are shielded by our strength, stamina and courage. We tolerate and accept the stress as routine weathering the storm offering a sigh of relief at its completion.

For some it is a hard blow, severe and devastating. Its victims unable to cope submerging them into a state of depression, isolation, withdrawal and low self-esteem, inflicting debilitation life threatening damage and consequences in its wake.

Hands tied feeling helpless, loved ones are at a loss in finding a solution seeking help through prayer, religion, church and counseling, possible psychiatry and intervention.

Caring and understanding support and commitment are the lifelines we share and extend to those we love and are in need.

We petition our Creator to diminish its impact and diffuse the force lying within all of us.

With a strong will, empowered mind and understanding, we stand firm in our resolve to wipe out this silent enemy called anxiety.

THE CLOCK

Tick Tock, Tick Tock
Minutes counting
Hands moving.

Moving slowly at a snail's pace in moments of anxiety, stress or fatigue
Time in motion its existence, space on the wall prominent and defined.
Waiting, waiting straining watching as it crawls around its circle.

Anxious, nerves hyper, a voice screaming within urging movement and speed
Tick Tock, Tick Tock the hour struck, its goal finally reached
The doctor will see you now.

Relief flows and ebbs within us erasing the restlessness and endless waiting.
Discomfort subsides a feeling of relief,
and weightlessness washes over us as the burden is lifted.

Our patience rewarded, the news joyous
uplifting our spirits, temperament and emotions.
We relax, our senses calm, we smile.

God is merciful and good
Thank you for His favor.

WAITING

How often do we find ourselves tapping our fingers, reading a magazine or just sitting waiting, waiting, and waiting.

If we were to research the amount of hours we spend waiting we would be shocked.

It seems as though a large percentage of our daily activities involve some form of waiting. There are many phases of waiting some as simple as boiling water, as complex as testing a computer program or acute anxiety waiting for results of a medical test or procedure.

What transpires during this down time? How do we tolerate the slow passage of time during this trial of our patience? I feel it depends on the reason, type and length of time it will take. Something very simple may involve insignificant thought while something more intense requires a test of will and stamina.

In my time of trial I pray. With rosary in my hand, I take solace in the feeling of the textured beads and the concentration of prayer, a spiritual respite and helpful distraction from watching the clock.

I am a worrier by nature, so for me waiting causes my anxiety level to rise. I am very stressed especially with results of medical tests. The people responsible for the delay are impervious to my worry and frustration. I don't know if they have become numb over the years or if they don't understand my irritation and annoyance, which only adds fuel to the existing turmoil within.

Some people are blessed with a no worry, relaxed attitude and find waiting just a nonchalant daily routine. I respect and understand their complacency, but on the other hand I envy their gift. I try to practice tolerance and patience and seem outwardly to be in control, but inwardly I am a mess.

I am very relaxed in traffic, cooking a time consuming dish, waiting for late guests; but when it comes to medical situations, I am a bunch of nerves. It seems my imagination runs amuck with the worst of each scenario. I am sure some would say I am being ridiculous and paranoid while others would sympathize and knowingly shake their heads in understanding. Regardless of other's opinions, waiting is a constant activity affecting our daily routine which forces us to adopt our psyche, control our emotions and present a calm and friendly façade to those around us. This is not an easy task by any stretch, but something we deal with as part of our nature and the complexity of our personality.

During this time of anxiety, I am reminded of a saying my mother is constantly telling me, "Daughter, it is all part of living, deal with it, look at me I am 87 years old and *I'm* still here".

"A respect for people whose age has given them wisdom."

CHAPTER 6

BEYOND MENOPAUSE

November sixteenth, the day I turned sixty was a day of unexplainable feelings bearing mixed emotions. On one hand happy to celebrate and on the other saddened at the fact I was getting older. Was I experiencing happiness, sadness or anxiety over things passed or yet to come, or is it just contentment or pure shock. I didn't feel old, although I don't know exactly how old is supposed to feel. There have been signs along the way for example, receiving an AARP card or the letter from GE my company/employer defining my retirement options.

There have been physical changes: a creaking and stiffness in the joints, standing in the pantry wondering what it was I wanted, or needing my batteries recharged more often. I hadn't connected the meaning and significance of all those signs and signals as indications of aging. I just assumed they were normal, routine with an occasional absentminded event. Could these changes dare I say be categorized as "senior moments?"

Turning fifty had very little effect on me. It was just another birthday. On the other hand, the words sixty years old sent me into a nervous spin, provoking my thoughts to send my brain into overdrive.

As an older individual, I found myself questioning my existence, accomplishment and lifestyle which, after much deliberation, I found unsatisfactory and boring. I asked myself what have I contributed to society and how has my presence on this earth made a difference?

There is a little nagging voice in my head repeating over and over "do something. Make some changes." I experienced a strong desire to leave a marker that denotes my existence on this earth, nothing monumental but a small significant deed to mark my presence.

I taught school for twenty-five years. I suppose that would qualify as a marker. I wanted to make sure my family remembered their roots, resulting in a family cookbook for the next generation defining family traditions, our Italian heritage and genealogy. Once I began writing the cookbook, I discovered I enjoyed capturing my thoughts on paper. The idea of putting pen to paper was a new experience which was very invigorating and fulfilling. I had no idea I could write as it was very difficult for me to write in school. Could this be the marker I am searching for? My instincts tell me not exactly. My gut feelings are not satisfied with this option. My family is important, but they will remember me in their hearts with memories of the past regardless of my accomplishments.

Are these writings a possible significance of my contribution to society? I am not sure. I was asked what was I going to do with my writings, and frankly I don't know where this will take me. They have provided me with an opportunity to vent my spleen, voice my anger and opinions and to bring closure to the loss of my parents. It is my sincere hope that whoever reads this book will identify and commiserate with the situations, circumstances and events I have experienced knowing there are other people who have been in the same boat. I want the reader to shake and nod their heads and say "That happened to me." Someone else has been down that road.

Wherever this quest leads me I hope that someday my name will ring a bell and someone will remember me and say "Yes, I knew Sofia McNellis; she was my teacher, aunt, friend, sister or just a nice person. She is the author of "It's Time to Remember."

WRITING

How do I explain this invasion of my sub-conscious?
Words, phrases, sentences swirling in my head
Bursting to be released from their captivity.
Unable to give an explanation of the why, how, when or where of it.

Am I losing "it' or gaining "it"?
It haunts me in sleep, creating a topic,
thoughts and content begging to be written, lest I forget.

Once begun, the words flow and ebb in rhythm from beginning to end
creating disbelief, amazement, and wonder by the finished product.

Surprises, fear and anxiety have crossed my mind
demanding a reason, purpose and cause for this epiphany.
Family, friends constantly ask questions of its title, destination and final
resting place.

A character flaw surfaced a desire for an immediate listener – somcone to give
feedback and comment, not so much for ego, but as a boost to continue and
not to be discouraged by doubt or fear of disapproval.

Enough time and energy has been spent searching and dissecting; this issue is
non-productive and uscless.

My mind made up so with willful determination of purpose, a non-stoppable
attitude. I am answering the call following my heart and listening to the voice
within writing what must be said; and for the rest, God's plan, my destiny will
pave the way and lead me where I need to go.

Thoughts

Instinctive, provoking, timely

Mind boggling, overwhelming

Decisions, major or minor

Suppressed, put aside, held over

Powerful, light, happy or sad

Mind in overdrive, working, gears in motion, wheels turning

Sexual, scholastic, funny

Joyous, awe inspiring, self centered, selfish, jealousy, angry

Self owned, responsible, hidden within, private

Voiced, shared at will, partial or complete

Informative, comforting, complimentary

Distinctive, unique, self possessed, no access

Stubborn, nasty, mean

Calculating, conniving, plotting

Direct, indirect, spoken, unspoken

A single idea, a flash, an item.

Thoughts

LISTENING

Thoughts, open minded, unencumbered, free of clutter

Ears perked, in tune, on standby, at attention, sharp

Senses aroused, alert, activated, set

Bodily techniques in high gear, ready, prepared

Children, people, voices talking, laughing, crying

Music playing, classical, rock, country, R & B, all varieties

Radio, TV, Boombox, CD, Tapes or Stereo

Cars, sirens, windows, doors

Rattling, clanging, honking

Dogs, cats, barking, growling, mewing

Shrills, screaming, yelling, shouting loud or softly spoken

Their pitch high or low muted, whispered

Wind, rain, thunder, lightening, nature's show and tell

Weird noises, strange, mysterious sounds in the air, on the ground filling space

All around here, there, everywhere

Important, frivolous, serious, funny

Stop, pay attention, take notice, focus

Silence, concentrate, hush, deliberate

Listen

CROSSROADS

Have you ever found yourself at a point in your life where you feel driven to jump out of the box. The need to break away from the ordinary expectations society deems appropriate for someone your age. Your thoughts and sleep are interrupted driving you on, energizing you to experience your dreams to move forward into a new and challenging arena. A need to test the waters, take them out for a spin and see where they will take you. The adrenaline rush is stimulating all your senses physical as well as mentally demanding you answer the what if, how to and where do I go questions. Your mind is working in overdrive pushing you to take action and put a silence to its demands. You are charged and ready to begin the process, establish a game plan, start to network, prioritize each step, brainstorm ideas with friends, set timelines, and firmly commit yourself to the task.

All your cards are on the table. You took the plunge, bought the ticket, the train is leaving the track, the wheels are in motion. Hang on tight the journey has begun. Each milestone each destination is leading you closer to fulfilling your ambitions and accomplishing your goals. Perseverance, courage and endurance, attributes required to travel the road follow the course and seize the moment. Don't slow down, don't stop; go, keep moving. Second thoughts and doubts are unacceptable. You must answer the call, meet your self-appointed expectations and revel in their satisfaction. You have no time for negative response and advice, "it is for your own good" etc. This type of counsel is insignificant, a hindrance and annoyance tempting you to deter from your quest.

We are in the middle of the crossroad promising life changing opportunities, achievements, satisfaction and success. We must remain diligent, dedicated to follow the path we have chosen, overcome the hurdles and obstacles whatever they may be and stay focused on the end result and maintain the courage to see it to fruition.

Whatever the outcome big or small, good or bad, is not an issue. We have given it a shot, tried our best and brought closure to the nagging questions within us. Our persona has transitioned. We are a better person empowered, smarter and more experienced for our efforts. We have come to realize age is just a number; there is no correct time or place until we determine the when where and how of things. We have assumed the responsibility of our lives. The power, choice and decision is accountable to no one but ourselves.

Our heart has led us down the road; our destiny has taken a turn. We have assumed the challenge and are headed to something new, mysterious, scary and oh so much fun. The joy and euphoria we are experiencing is indescribable, energizing and stimulating giving us an intellectual high beyond words.

Guts or no guts, yes or no, walk forward or remain stagnant the choice is yours!!!

Book prologue change guts line to: Thus the birth of "It's Time to Remember".

"Mediocrity is the Enemy of Excellence"

Spoken individually they are simple straightforward words, but strung together they are complex, meaningful, thought provoking, reflective and possibly life changing. They question our goals, motivation, drive and way of life. They demand answers to difficult questions wondering whether this phrase applies to us, if so, are we inspired to take action?

Are we in a rut? Have we become stagnant, disinterested with each day rolling into the next taken for granted, uneventful and boring? Have we as a society become complacent, lazy, tired and old settling for the middle of the road without aspiration toward the better? Are we content with acceptance that this is the way it is or do we seek improvement? Do we blindly follow rules, regulations, restrictions and commands without understanding their meaning and consequence? Do we ask questions seeking explanation, application and understanding? Do we take a back seat, cower in a corner allowing someone else to take charge of our affairs? Do we accept defeat or do we go down fighting?

Questions, questions, questions rolling around, tumbling, seeking, imploring recognition and answers. What, where and how do we find the answers? Do we fit this category? Think, think, search, seek, find them from within, for they are part of ourselves, our make up and personality of who we are and want to be imploring us to stand up and focus on each day. Face it as a new experience bursting with excitement, creativity and challenge energizing us to accomplish simple and difficult tasks, compete with the opposition, set new goals staying alert, alive and active, being someone with accountability, a person to be reckoned with. A person who is appreciated and respected for who we are and what we do.

Are you the enabler or the enabled, the doer or the doormat? Passive or aggressive?

THE JOURNEY

It is not an easy task to describe this vocabulary word because of the infinite meaning and possibilities it denotes.

It can be happy or sad, meaningful or funny.

Is its path marred with tragedy, sorrow and pain, or is it joyous and wonderful?

Whatever the cause and effect, it is the road we must follow either by choice or necessity.

It is a calling higher than us, life changing beyond our understanding, a part of our being and existence here on earth.

The road is filled with obstacles, some simple others difficult; we must follow it nonetheless.

Sometimes the outcome is scary, frightening, unknown and unexpected pushing us forward; the walk heavy, long and motionless, with fear the driver.

On the other hand it can be surprising and pleasurable our feet dancing with gaiety and frivolity.

Regardless of the time, place and reason, the nature and composition of our being forces us to follow its direction regardless of the hardships, pitfalls, strife and anxiety.

The finish lends a feeling of closure and satisfaction, or sadly, consequences beyond our control depressing, down trodden and sad.

Armed with trepidation, determination, and faith in our hearts, we follow HIM, His hand on our shoulder, His footprints in the sand. We focus our energy on God's chosen path life's destiny as we travel the road, the journey reaching the final destination our heavenly reward.

Life is the journey, not the destination.

PICTURES

A blank wall spacious, white, open,

Reproductions of loved ones, their identity, emotion and activity begging for space.

Creative juices flowing, a timely opportunity for show, form and pride.

Geometric shapes, sizes, black, white or color; framed fancy or plain.

Scattered photos everywhere posed, candid, free lance; haphazard images to be arranged and sorted.

Memories of special events, times passed, loved ones randomly hung or patterned, awaiting their special niche displayed in a special place.

Their purpose, scene or cause is subject to public scrutiny, criticism, praise and fame. Their image does not change, it remains the same in content and design.

The wall is a complete collage of happenings, scenery, people and places on display for public eyes. Passive or aggressive, deliberate or at a quick glance, fast or slow; whatever the pace, they are enjoyable, mind boggling, thought provoking and reflective shared by the many. Cameras are ready to capture public reactions and comments. They are awed and inspired by the level and quality of the talent on display.

A cursory glance hurried without thought cheats the viewer providing minimal focus or memory of the image with little appreciation of its work and composition.

Pictures speak from within, their character flaws are hidden, secret and private lending a sense of mystery and intrigue. The critics dissect, analyze and judge their purpose, vision and beauty.

Intense participation of the subject's theme, message and story provide an opportunity to participate in a slow, deliberate look and study of all their details and nuances, whereby the viewer is aesthetically rewarded for their time spent.

An array of topics which are happy, bright, morose or sad are displayed symmetrically, its geometric design unusual and unique.

The old adage rings true, "A picture is worth a thousand words."

THE SANCTUARY

Niche, small room, closet, corner, hideaway
Secret, obscure, hidden, remote, silent.

A place to chill, relax, calm oneself, sleep, escape
Meditation, prayer, sorting thoughts, reflection, writing, its purpose defined.

Sitting, standing, reclining or stretched out
Comfortable, warm, inviting, pleasant, soothing.

Visitors, phone calls, interruptions, disturbances annoying, unwelcome
Solitude, quiet, peaceful moments stolen, rented constrained by time.

Memories recalled, stories read, journals written, words of worship voiced
Remembrances, reminiscence, recollections past and present.

Tears of sadness soft, muted, whispered
Laughter, giggles, smiles, sounds of joy and happiness.

A wondrous place hushed, cherished, revered
Solely owned, personal, confidential, private.

Solid, strong, inviting, beckoning, calling
Singular to one's self, exceptional, rewarding, challenging.

The sanctuary!

PRIVACY

A closed door, a quiet spot, a hidden place

Alone, by oneself, solitude

Words, thoughts, meditated, unspoken

Held close to the breast, within the heart, touching the soul

Feelings and emotions too personal, intense, revealing

Peace, calm, solace, consolation, comfort

Privacy

"Take time to energize the body and renew the spirit."

CHAPTER 7

ENJOYING THE MOMENT

Dawn is rising. The sunlight is peeking through the clouds shining through my window, brightening the room, caressing my face, touching my eyes, signaling the beginning of a new day. One eye opens, then another, a reminder to check the time. Does my slumber continue or is it time to rise and begin a new day?

My morning is activated and set into motion. All parts of my body awaken, commencing with a visit to the bathroom, sneezing, eyes tearing, coughing, grumbling and yawning. As a pre-senior citizen, I cannot quickly rise out of bed and jumpstart the day. I need to sit up in bed for at least 15 to 20 minutes in order to gear up the body parts, check my brain for any malfunctions, ask if a grease job is required and see what pain remedy and pills are needed for the day. Once the body is purring and the engine is running, I focus on my plans and activities for the day. I begin with my prayers of thanks for all the gifts and blessings God has bestowed on me and mine. I list my petitions asking Him, Padre Pio and all the saints for the health and safety for all those on my prayer list. I thank Him for uplifting my spirit, calmimg my anxiety and relaxing my emotions as I pray.

As I make the bed, straighten the room, gather my clothes and head for the shower fully dressed, my day officially has begun. It is beautiful, alive and energized, inviting me to participate, soak up its warmth and enjoy it, promising me an active and productive schedule appreciative of God's wonderful gift.

I cannot foresee what each day will bring or how my life and destiny will change, but today I am alive, ready to move, shake and go. Wow, I feel good! Thanks God for today; I will make you proud.

The day was clean and bright, promising temperatures in the seventies. Suddenly I heard myself repeating the same mantra over and over "Do I have to go to work; do I really have to go?"

My spirit was not willing; my flesh was definitely weak tempting me with images of a day of enjoyment, shopping and having lunch with friends, but my common sense ruled out. As I pulled into the parking lot, three co-workers arrived at the same time and pulled up alongside of me. Imagine the shock and amazement evident on our faces over such a coincidence. All seemed reluctant to exit their car pretending to gather belongings, adjusting the seat and delaying the inevitable.

Annoyed and groaning, I made my move. Greetings said, all commented in unison on how hard it was to come to work on such a wonderful day, all in agreement it should have been a day of rest and relaxation (R&R). All at once it seemed as though a huge light bulb was shining above our heads flashing don't go in; take a vacation day.

Decision made, we climbed into my mini-van, drove to the nearest phone and called our boss, inventing lame excuses for our absence. As the last caller, our boss instructed me to have the others listen as we heard him say, "Have a good time; see you tomorrow." Our conscience satisfied, happily we headed down the shore for the day, wondering if he had ESP.

Till this day as I reflect upon this memory, I remember our faces, and I can't believe how spontaneous and fearless we were, giggling and talking, glowing with pride and still numb with shock that on the spur of the moment just like that we played hooky from work. Thank goodness we had a caring and understanding boss.

While we were planning the day's schedule, we heard a loud, embarrassing abdominal/bowel sound echoing in the confines of the car. Manners dictated the pretense of ignorance and bad hearing, but we knew the cause and I was glad it was someone else.

Incident forgotten, a sense of quiet fell over us; our thoughts busy in anticipation of the day's outing. Out of the blue, a voice sounded from the backseat of the car breaking into our silence disturbing our reverie echoing these wonderful words, as my grandmother said, "Wherever you be, let your wind go free." Truer words were never spoken in more ways than one.

The memory of this day reminds me that life is too short that it is okay to deviate from the ordinary routine and break away once in a while to listen to your gut and go for it. The memory of that day has given me joy over the years a release from the stress and anxiety we often experience. I remember my co-workers and the cameradie and good times we shared that day. I often wonder where they are and how they are doing.

When my days are hectic and time my enemy, I remember that day and the freedom and pride I felt in myself for making that decision to follow my instinct and enjoy. I have gained comfort and strength from that experience to continue and follow through my actions and decisions. Several times during my lifetime I have designated a day here and there as an R&R day, an opportunity to do whatever comes to my mind. The experience has taught me that it is okay to occasionally care for oneself. We work hard taking care of others and doing what is necessary to survive, so we are entitled to act upon our whims without guilt or consequence. The result is a healthier outlook, increased energy and a darn good time.

SHOES

Leather, vinyl, plastic or wooden
Loafers, moccasins, sneakers, sandals or flops
Laced, velcro, buckles or straps
High heels, low heels, wedged or flat.

Smelly or fresh their function the same
Vinyl or rubber the soles are made
Big or small a size for all
Tied or untied, opened or closed.

Reebok, Gucci, Florsheim, whoever designed
Sized to perfection or maybe not
Comfortable and snug, loose or tight
Energized and ready to take flight.

Dancing, jumping, or running to town
Whatever purpose or task
Coming or going, stepping out or in
That old adage resounds.

These shoes are made for walking, that's what they do!!

A Nice Day

Sun shining its reflection bright

Blue sky, clouds puffy and white

Birds flying landing on the sand noisy, loud

Umbrellas dancing, swaying in the breeze

Blue water lapping against the sand

An atmosphere relaxed peaceful and calm

People riding bikes, jogging, walking, surveying the beach

Sounds of the ocean filling the air

Hustle, bustle, shopping, admiring the goods

In and out the shops in the mall

Homemade fudge, salt water taffy, lemonade and bottled water

Time spent happy, savored and appreciated

Memories made of family and friends

A nice day, compliments of God.

SHOPPING

Hustle, Bustle
In, Out
This way, that way
Up down, down up, Up down
Hurry here, hurry there
Pick up one then another
Is it the right size or color?
Coupon or sale item
Cash or charge
Decisions, decisions, decisions
What should I do?
Temperature rising, body too hot
Standing in line after line
Waiting your turn
Patience strained
Bag or box, Wrap or not
More to go, on a roll
No stopping, must get done
End is near
Scan the list
Checkout is over
Rush to car
Where is it parked?
Think, remember where
Feet hurt, arms sore
All is done
A sigh of relief and accomplishment
Task complete
Wrapping awaits
The cycle repeats!
Shopping

The Time is Now

Is now the time for me to face facts, take stock and face reality?

Is it time for me to gather my thoughts, take inventory, review my status and execute my dreams and ambitions?

Is my age demanding I switch gears, deviate from following the standard pattern and usual routine and stop coasting along the unchallenged and boring highway?

The world is changing. Are the new age renditions passing me by? What am I missing, and how will I be able to fit in if I don't pay attention to my heart and participate in this revolution?

Am I feeling the challenge and driven by the need for something new and different?

What is the meaning and philosophy that I want my retirement to reflect?

These questions are profound carrying with them a series of heavy thinking, planning, action and execution.

Where do I want to spend my senior years?

Are my finances solid enough to allow me options and choices for upgrading and improving my current residence, status and way of life?

Is it time to review my health issues to lose weight, exercise and eat healthy in order to survive my retirement?

Positively, certainly, yes my time is now. My list is formulating in my head as I write. I can't put the words to paper quick enough. It is my time to focus on my own needs, dreams, ambitions and accomplishments. I must make the decisions and choices based on what, where and how I want my life to be. I need to consider my feelings, focus on who I am and follow through with my convictions. My mind is made up, my goals are set and I am ready to set them into motion and watch them take flight.

I must tap into my resources of courage and strength, fortify my guts and plunge forward head on with the determination to overcome whatever obstacles or hurdles come my way.

I want my life to continue to count for something, to dedicate my space and time to sharing my knowledge and experiences with others to help them with their difficulties, decisions and choices so that they understand how significant and important their lives on this earth are. Their presences **have** meaning, intent and purpose, their contribution to society a boon to those around them.

Bragging, gloating, the pinning of medals and blowing of the horns are not part of the script. Perhaps my twenty years of teaching have led me to this point. I sincerely want to help out in whatever way I can to share what I have learned, and maybe I can make a difference in someone's life.

I cannot take full credit for this volcanic explosion of energy I am experiencing. A caring heart, a listening ear, her unfaltering confidence and belief and forceful spirit have brought me to this moment. Cuz, you have done it again! I offer you my sincere gratitude and thanks.

I want to experience personal satisfaction for my life choices and achieve what I set out to do. I will make you proud. I want my epitaph, the final chapter to read: "She made use of the gifts God bestowed upon her. She shared them with others according to His will."

Priorities

Circumstances and events from the previous holidays have conjugated serious questions demanding I dig deep within myself to find the answers and attempt to understand their hurtful punch in order to provide me with an emotional release. Vulnerable and unprotected I experienced a life changing soul searching transition where heartfelt desire and intent toward me had transformed into duty and obligation.

Old-fashioned tradition is considered "old age thinking" replaced by the "new age way". Caring, concern and good deeds toward others have been put aside to be replaced by multiple items scheduled on an over prioritized list.

Phone calls, human contact and communication and the sending of cards have become fleeting momentary thoughts forgotten in an instant, replaced by trips to the store or the next project or chore. Calls to family and friends have become infrequent even non-existent, a low priority, substituted by emails and electronic technology, a cold and unfriendly quick fix. Sadly the recipient is unaware that he or she were even remembered in that moment. Apologies, sorry become old and mundane and more difficult to accept. Missed events and occasions, canceling meetings, luncheons become the norm rather than the occasional.

We help those in need by sending a check or cash in order to satisfy ones conscience, duty and guilt. Funerals, illness and emergency situations arc squeezed into the schedule offering limited time for consolation categorized as an annoyance, something that has to be done.

Spirituality, faith, religious duty practiced only when needed, left out of the daily routine, observed only on holidays and main events due to obligation or guilt. Meditation on values, integrity, morality and matters of daily living are unscheduled thought and contemplation, their intent and meaning hurried and rushed, time interrupted by the demands of progress.

How often do we express interest, concern or caring for no reason, no ulterior motive of a just because? Outward grief, sharing memories of deceased loved one considered "old age thinking" replaced by the "new age" which demands a letting go, moving on a closure to memories and experiences shut off, not to be reminisced or discussed, tolerated by the listener only "if it makes the person feel better."

My beliefs and faith will not permit me to deny a loved one's spiritual presence and identity to bury them forever and totally erase their existence. Family and friends hold our precious gifts of unconditional love and trust. When compromised it strikes out and attacks our vulnerability causing untold hurt and pain to our emotions and heart. The scars run deep severing our emotional bond causing distrust and disbelief, requiring time for repair and restitution.

The world has changed, our way of life compromised, challenged beyond reason. Our ability for survival demanding impossible social, financial and family responsibilities, more difficult to offer commitment, our relationships, friendships, health and job security threatened, sacrificed.

This lack of thought is similar to a cancer creeping slowly within eating away what we believe in and hold dear to our hearts. Is this an instrument of the devil stealing away our hope and joy? Sadly and ironically there is no deliberate underlying anger, meanness or malice intended. It is the result of focusing and concentrating on outside stumuli gone out of control.

These facts are very frightening and horrific to comprehend this "new age" way of life depriving us of expectations, accomplishments and success. We are constantly juggling dates unable to stay on track frustrated, stressed out with insufficient time to complete the task, having to prioritize, neglecting and disappointing others and ourselves.

Is this the legacy we want for the future generation? Are these the values that we wish to impart to them? Do we find this acceptable or do we justify it as reality and the way things are? Are we willing to run the risk of losing our friends and family ties, the core of the past, present and future of our existence and destiny.

It is time to say NO, to take inventory, get back to basics and resurrect our memories for us to enjoy and revel in them. Vow to create moments and events to be stored in the treasure chest of our heart to be passed on so that our identity, our very person will be remembered with kindness and a smile.

Priorities, agendas, lists are important tools for organization but must be maintained within reasonable parameters, flexibility and consideration of one's physical and mental limitations.

We cannot change the world, but we must take control of our life, follow God's Plan, become our own boss and establish a unique and personal "so called age" for ourselves, make a commitment and stand by our convictions.

BOREDOM

What is boredom? Is it idle time? Mindless work, a precursor to depression, monotony, or just nothing to do?

What are the symptoms? Staring into space, a blank look, yawning, tapping something, constant eating, watching the clock, lack of a challenge or tedium with a job or task?

What are the causes? Physical disability, type of work, loneliness, laziness?

How does the victim recognize the affliction? Is the person tired, listless, sleepy, unphased with time and space?

Regardless of the characteristics, the effects are the same. They are overpowering, a gradual take over of the body, a subtle change in thinking and over time they become an albatross depleting mental force, activity, drive and spirit leading into the norm rather than the occasional.

What is the cure? An attitude change, new job, breaking away from routine day in day out activities, determination of spirit, redirected energy, self-confidence, a new pastime, hobby or routine.

In theory, any or all of the above will spark the spirit and ignite the power from within the psyche only if the victim is motivated and willing to take charge, affect change and defeat the enemy.

Whatever the cause or solution, action is crucial. He or she must define their individual purpose in order to stand up and fight to take command and begin the change. Whether it is big or small, drastic or simple, they have acknowledged the problem, their mind set, upon doing whatever it takes to succeed. Their spirit will be revitalized creating a new energy for themselves and those who share their space.

"Truth is truth. Nobody believes it.
Error is error. Everyone thinks it's right."

Bishop Fulton J. Sheen

CHAPTER 8

Two Sets of Eyes

My parents remained embedded in the traditions and customs of their parents and lived a simple life. They were steadfast in practicing their Catholic religion; their hard work, integrity, honesty and moral codes were the foundation that provided a solid environment for them to raise their family.

Their door was always open to anyone who came to visit. Everyone was accepted at face value. The color of their skin, nationality or financial status was of no consequence. All were treated with respect and entertained with good food and generous hospitality.

My parents maintained the philosophy that wherever adults were engaged in drink and conversation it was not a place for children's eyes and ears. We were sent out to play and told to stay close to the house where we could be seen.

My brother and I were not exposed to unlawful behavior, fights and cursing. We were protected from witnessing that type of activity. My parents followed the straight and narrow lifestyle, keeping busy with their daily routine, performing chores and providing the basic food and shelter for their home and family.

Over the years, times changed and my parents experienced many hard times of betrayal, hurt and disappointment. Oddly, my mother was more intuitive than my father. She could look into someone's eyes and see their true personality. She believed in dreams and would have premonitions about the past, present and future happenings. She and my cousin, Jo, would share the same insights and attributes. They would interpret dreams and discuss their meaning and effects. I was the skeptic in the family and did not believe in any of their visions and used to tease them many times. I must admit that they have been right on target more times than none.

I am a type of person who has to learn the hard way, needing to experience something before I get the message. Over the years, I have had my share of cruel unkind actions, extreme hurt, embarrassment and disappointment because I failed to look beyond the obvious.

When I was in my late twenties, I was engaged to be married in June of 1969. At the time I was teaching second grade in a Catholic school. In April of that year, the faculty, parents and students planned a bridal shower for me. Two weeks before the shower, I received a call from my fiancés mother, informing me that her son did not want to get married and I was to cancel the wedding.

Imagine the shock, betrayal, hurt and rejection I felt to hear those words and realize he didn't have the courtesy or the guts to tell me in person. I had to cancel the arrangements forfeiting the down payments, reimburse the bridesmaids for their gowns and return all the engagement gifts with a letter of apology. Making the phone call to the school cancelling the shower was so humiliating and embarrassing, especially having to face the children everyday. They were understanding, caring and giving and helped me to handle and survive the episode.

Three years passed and I happened to be in the bank when I saw my ex fiancé walk through the door. Initially I didn't recognize him his hair was dyed blonde and his clothes were unusual. I couldn't believe my eyes. He was holding hands with his gay companion and suddenly the secret of the mystery came to light. He cancelled the wedding because of his sexual preference. On one hand, it was a bitter pill to swallow but on the other, I was relieved to know that I was not responsible. It is true that God works in mysterious ways. I was given closure to a question that was on my mind for a long time. I should have paid attention to the signs along the way-the conversations, behavior and little nuances that would have given me an inkling into his personality. Later, I found out he was discharged from the service for his chosen lifestyle.

In a way, I blame my protected upbringing and religious beliefs for my naïve and innocent outlook and the way I view the people I encounter. I believed in people and what they portrayed without questioning or doubting their words.

Many times in our life all of us have experienced episodes and events that have caused us to learn the hard way, suffering injury to our ego and personality. My mother and cousin were correct in looking beneath the surface to carefully pay attention and listen to what is going on around them and to follow their instincts.

As I write this chapter, memories of a story my grandmother told me enter my thoughts. My grandmother and grandfather had recently moved into their first house in a little street in South Philadelphia, Pa. They scrimped and saved every penny to buy that house-it was a big event in their lives. Grandpop was a chimney sweep who worked long hours to provide for his wife and their four children. Grandmom kept the house and did odd jobs whenever she could.

My grandfather's sister lived a few blocks from them and did not like my grandmother. She could not have any children, and her envy and jealousy overpowered and consumed her. She would go to my grandmother's house and bang on the door, shouting vile insults and screaming for all the neighbors to hear. My grandmother would not open the door and ignored her until she would get tired and go away. Her visits were becoming more frequent and violent, forcing my grandmother to do something to end the situation. The next time her sister-in-law came to visit my grandmother opened the door and confronted her. She smacked my grandmother in the face and my grandmother grabbed her arms and pinned her to the wall and voiced these words "Someday, you will not be able to close your eyes in death unless you see my face." Those words frightened her and she never returned.

Three years later, a woman came banging on my grandmother's window. She said "Your sister-in-law is dying and is screaming your name and cannot close her eyes." My grandmother grabbed her shawl and went to her house. She held her hand, offered her forgiveness and stayed with her until she closed her eyes in the final moments of her life.

Recollections of my mother and grandmother have taught me to see things with two sets of eyes. Without rhyme, reason or excuse, I can sense and feel other people's karma and the evil they possess. I see blackness in their eyes and suddenly I get the chills and my body turns very cold. Initially, I was frightened out of my wits but then I remembered my mom and my cousin and their premonitions and realized this was very similar to what they experienced. This extra sense is a gift given to me that has protected me against the evil manipulation and con evil people practice. It has prevented me from falling prey to their evil ways. I do not purport to judge or label anyone. My feelings are strictly private within myself and not for public knowledge.

Thus far, there have only been two people whom I sensed as truly evil. My mother used to say that they made a pact with the devil. They were mean and manipulative, ending friendships and relationships with their lies. They told untrue degrading stories and spread rumors, causing rifts in families and stealing money from the elderly. No matter how much evil and destruction they leave in their wake, they end up triumphant. My mother and I would discuss this dilemma, shaking her head, she explained. "Daughter, when the time comes for them to pay back the devil, they fight it and don't want to go, but it is too late before they wise up." They have an unreasonable desire to learn, hear and know all things that are bad for us. They choose to live in the darkness of evil rather than follow the light of salvation.

God has given us the option of choice. We can choose a good life of prosperity or an evil life of death and doom. The choice bears rewards, consequences and accountability.

PENALTIES VS. REWARDS

Penalties

Unkind, wrong doing, unlawful

Abused, harmful, misused

Willful, planned, accidental, mishap

Judged, cited, fined, sentenced

Victim, circumstance, act

Pay back, restitution, time spent.

Rewards

Kindness, good deed, actions

Traded, swapped, monetary, material

Voluntary, spur of the moment, thoughtful

Friends, games, scholastic, sports, hard work

Chance, gamble, lucky, worthwhile, good feeling.

Opposite entities, bearing responsibility, behavior accountability, demanding results.

The pendulum swings one good the other bad.

Penalties verses Rewards.

AGGRAVATION

A long word comprised of eleven letters, nasty and mean; its origin complex, sneaky, deliberate and spiteful. It is a word bearing devious cause and effect buried deep down beneath the surface building within, like water simmering ready to boil rising to a crescendo exploding into many fragments.

It is designed to agitate, stress, and injure while severely intensifying the blow like pulling the trigger of a gun, its victims unaware of the when, where and how of it.

It is not discriminatory, takes no prisoners. It is silently creeping, crawling causing havoc in the body, nerves on edge, screaming sending a hard punch to the stomach; the recipient ready to lose control at the breaking point.

Driving in heavy traffic, intense paperwork, an inexcusable action, arguing, waiting in endless lines, a bad day. All situations prime, designed to cause tension, anger, fists in a ball, stomach rolling, all in motion ready to respond.

Swallowing hard, walking away shaking one's head, all methods of self-protection. We must develop a shield of armor strong, solid, impenetrable, protective for if left unmanaged, unchecked it will fester continuing to cause damage leaving a trail of anger, frustration and poor health in its wake.

No matter how often or how many ways we try to combat this dangerous silent enemy, it continues to gain momentum causing pent up feelings, aggression, words left unsaid, satisfaction unabated.

Aggravation.

UNACCEPTABLE

Have I been sleepwalking, dreaming, in a trance, catatonic or just oblivious to the people in my space?

When did I become aware of the persona of human beings, their habits, nature, feelings and beliefs?

Has maturity awakened me from a deep sleep resulting in an ability to understand, detect and view things through a different perspective using experienced wiser eyes? My recent insight this new vision, rude awakening, however explained sucks.

Reality TV, radio talk shows, current times and people are hawking realities that in my opinion, are depressing, frightening and downright scary. They are depicting characters that are out of the box, beyond the norm, who believe and accept life with indifference and disrespect for each other and the law.

Several examples come to mind that I have personally witnessed and wish to elaborate.

- Drug abuse, violence, murder part of the everyday life in many neighborhoods.
- Cheating partners in a relationship, women sharing sex and children with the same man paying his bills, new car, spending money and place to live.
- Tattoos on breasts made visible to tease and entice onlookers sending signals to employers/employees of their sexuality.
- Colored armbands boasting teenage sexual conquests.
- A co-worker announces the birth of her granddaughter in one breath and the need for a DNA test to determine the race and paternity of the child with next.
- People faking serious illness and severely exaggerating their symptoms in order to slack off on the job, gain sympathy and attention.
- Children inflicting insults, mockery, often ignoring each other, the professional in charge too busy to notice.

Throughout the years, such behavior was considered deplorable, intolerable, illegal and sinful. Currently it is dealt with complacency, disrespect, tolerance and acceptance. When did the metamorphous occur switch, changeover, this change in attitude? How did such atrocities become acceptable? Was it slow and gradual or fast and quick, and how did it take over and become the norm? What happened to the belief in a code of ethics, moral integrity and morality? Fear, disappointment, astonishment and disbelief have registered I am offended and outraged.

The world has changed. There is no love, caring and respect for one's own self. Is it time to build another ark? How can God witness such a lack of shame, remorse, privacy, spirituality and goodness from his creation and not be devastated and saddened?

We, the majority must be strong in our faith, use the tools provided by our religious beliefs and fight the virus that threatens our world spreading the good news from door to door, person to person shouting, screaming this is unacceptable. Majority or Minority your choice!

GOSSIP

Shush, don't tell anyone, keep this to yourself, did you hear about so and so.........................

The Bait: Introductory verbiage capturing our attention, arousing curiosity, sharpening our hearing and sending our antennae into overdrive.

Words on the hook—bated and submerged plunging us deep into a sticky situation—an uncomfortable conundrum vulnerable to its allure, repercussions, bite and consequences.

Do we instinctively satisfy the urge or morally reject the temptation with ears burning curiosity unabated?

Once spoken the venom gains momentum traveling faster than a speeding bullet, powerful and more lethal than a loaded shotgun. It strikes the target invading one's privacy leaving abuse and mental destruction in its wake taking no prisoners.

No kidding, really, oh my, I can't believe it, really.........................

The Hook: Reactionary recantations of surprise and shock setting into motion countless reactions and speculation, scoring serious retributions and side effects upon its subject.

There are various types of secrets some cruel, condescending, criticizing and others that are stupid and annoying.

Reeled in: As victims, they "impart" a sharp blow to the stomach causing our psyche and emotions to recoil from the force and shock of pain.

Remorse: In hindsight has anything been proven or changed by this unproductive participation in jealousy, spitefulness and unkind behavior toward humanity? Often times we don't see the direct results of the damage incurred by the spoken words because the recipient puts on a nonchalant façade appearing to be non-pulsed by the event, but we know better.

Downstream: Mission accomplished; the perpetrator has moved on to the next conspirator spreading lies and stories like manure. Its recipients are left with the rumors pressed up against their lips, bursting to be released from captivity fighting a troubled conscience agonizing over the right and wrong of its content and effects.

What started out as a nice day has turned into ruination and ugliness. Such are the trials and tribulations of that six letter word known as gossip that packs such a punch to the solar plexus shouting and spreading vulgarity and lies throughout the room, its path leaving guilt and destruction along the way.

An Unkind Remark

You're fat, you need to lose weight, you eat too much.......

Words offered for advice obviously to someone the giver deems to be overweight/fat.

What criteria, rhyme, reason or circumstance determined this statement?

Was it through observation perceived by a friend or family member offered as a gesture of kindness and concern, or having lunch while all are complaining and discussing their eating habits, or as medical advice in a professional, caring manner in conjunction with diet, helpful techniques and follow up sessions?

Unfortunately there are those who have formulated opinions that are prejudiced and derogatory toward overweight/obese people. It is not a foregone conclusion that someone who is overweight overeats, pigs out or lacks control. There are many factors and circumstances that contribute to one's size and appearance. For some, prescription drugs have serious side effects causing enormous weight gain, a physiological condition or glandular problem, all a possibility of the cause.

Thoughtless comments said privately or publicly are unkind, hurtful and oblivious to the recipient's mood or situation prevalent at the time. Not understood or realized is the subject's awareness of the image reflected inside and outside the mirror.

Outward appearance can be deceiving and should not be taken for granted and assumed.

Consideration and respect must be uppermost in our minds formulating the thought process into thinking before speaking.

Helpful advice can be given in a caring, gentle and sometimes humorous form, acknowledging and recognizing the personality and acceptance of the remarks from the person.

We have all criticized and chastised ourselves for eating too many treats and started dieting and exercising, losing the weight and gaining it back. Sometimes we slip and forget these times.

Remember them, for we all have Been there, Done That!!

PERCEPTION

One word,
multiple descriptions
universal, influential, effective.

Opinions, understanding, interpretation, concept and outlook its drivers.
Digested, believed, formulated, unique and single owned,
hard to change, solid and steadfast.

Bias, prejudice, misuse, dangerous,
possible cause and effects passed on to continue.

Strong, powerful, influential, eyes, ears, mouth
the carriers verbal or written;
however given, its message delivered cunning and unsuspected.

Caution, care, delicacy, consideration and thought,
essential elements when shared and expounded,
its recipients carefully selected.

Perceived or perceiving,
observed or recognized,
its expression powerful,
Perception.

THE MIRROR

Square, round, oval, diamond geometric

Various shapes, many sizes and angles

Framed, unframed, fancy or plain, with design or not

Stand, pose, look and see

Make a face, laugh or cry

Self image, true reflection, without lies

No gimmicks, substitutes, or changes

Untouched, erased or deleted

A looking glass, shining and clear.

The mirror!

CAPACITY

My weekly routine is comprised of work (3 days a week), occasional doctor's visits, shopping, lunch with friend's etc. etc. As a result I am constantly exposed to all sorts and types of people, places and situations – listening, learning and hearing stories, comments, news and current events, their cause and effects discussed and analyzed.

On such an occasion while discussing the movie "The Passion of Christ", someone asked me "who was Jesus Christ and what is the Passion?" At the time of the Pope's death, the question came up as to whether the Pope was married and how many children did he have? I had to refrain from keeping my mouth open and shaking my head as I answered their questions.

Newspapers, books, articles are filled with facts and information covering the events, but these activities are not part of their time allotment or schedule; it is for others, not themselves. Sadly they are uninspired, uninterested, and their curiosity levels limited to the present and immediate time zone. They respond without forethought and are quick to judge outward appearance, their primary criteria. They have yet to realize that looks and chronological age are deceiving. Experience and knowledge is power.

One chilly day I chose to wear corduroy pants and was immediately informed that it was spring and corduroy was out, but it was ok for me because I was old.

On another occasion while discussing a recent crime event, I made the comment "there is more there than meets the eye" and heard, "say it real, what did you mean?"

If I use words with more than six letters, the listeners have no concept of their meaning or context. I'm told, "We are not into the big words".

They are unable to make change, calculate numbers without the aide of a computer. The list is endless.

As a teacher, as a cognizant being, I am flabbergasted and fully taken back by the lackadaisical, nonchalant attitude apparent in the younger members of society.

They are not getting dumber. Their minds are in overload inhibiting their ability to comprehend, deduct and assimilate facts, the rhyme or reason of things. They lack respect for the past and present. Their energy, drive and ambition is focused in too may directions scattered and unorganized. They lack the capacity to get it, and unfortunately if gotten, relate and store it as an experience for the future.

My intent is not to bash anyone or group, and I apologize for being so blunt and venting my opinions. I feel something is broken and needs to be fixed. Lack of knowledge is not only dangerous but also scary.

CAN YOU HEAR ME?

Mission: Simple task; place liner into wastebasket whenever needed.

Can you hear me? Do you understand? Words repeated, many times they become a daily mantra. They remind me of a commercial for a popular cell phone depicting a guy traveling the globe saying "can you hear me" over and over testing the device's communication level and engineering capacity.

Can you hear me? Do you understand? Spoken to recipient to open dialog for conversation. Their response a blank stare, speaker decides to change sentences, focus in another direction, use synonyms for the same words, scramble them into a different format, then repeat them. Response, a negative shake of head. Repeat them again and again in several ways. The frustration level is building on both ends. Words not working, think, think; figure it out, choose another option. Remember the pigeons, stimulus, response, show and tell; that is it, give it a try. Physically demonstrate the task, show it by example.

Can you see it? Do you understand? Response hand waved, attention dismissed, listening shut down. Process repeated over course of several days without words patiently directed. Give it a chance; allow time for practice and accomplishment.

Surprise: Understanding incomplete; task unsuccessful. A simple task impossible to convey.

Questions: How can it be? All attempts and options exhausted, tried and failed. Is it a test of will? Is it because the person is mentally incapable of understanding and following direction or is it because the person is being single minded, obstinate, stubborn, playing games, unwilling to cooperate?

Did the person understand? Has the person heard the words? Is it playing games or not? Benefit of doubt, yes or no? Stubborn or incapable? Don't know, not sure? Don't know; just don't know.

Mission: incomplete, stymied. Patience and frustration level stressed out.

Enough, done. Wastebasket empty!

"Kind words are like honey—enjoyable and healthful."

An old proverb

A Quiet Voice

Throughout this book, I have told stories of my parents and how they raised our family. We had very strict rules that warranted no deviation. We were trained to keep quiet and to think before we speak. If someone was wearing a funny outfit, we had to remain neutral and not show any disrespect toward the way they dressed.

My father's family lived in Italy and wanted to join their brother in America, the land of opportunity and prosperity. My father filed the necessary paperwork and called for his sisters to come to the USA. It was not an easy process because each sponsor had to provide each immigrant with a place to live, a job and had to guarantee the individuals practiced and obeyed the law. It took over twenty years for them to come over to this country. My Aunt her husband and their two children, Peter and Loretta, arrived in the spring and although a little cramped they lived with us. We were very excited to meet and learn all about our roots in Italy. They lived with us for two years until they saved enough money to get their own apartment. Eventually with hard work and sacrifice, they were able to leave the apartment and buy a little house in a few towns away.

I will never forget the time they invited us to a home-style Italian dinner in their new house. Our taste buds were bouncing just thinking about all the wonderful dishes we were going to eat. In the Italian tradition, a typical Italian meal began with holiday soup, antipasto salad, pasta with (gravy meat, meatballs, sausage and pork ribs) followed by a roasted chicken, potatoes, broccoli rabe, ending with fruit and nuts for dessert. Pastries and sweets are reserved for special occasions. Homemade wine was always in abundance and the drink of choice.

As soon as we arrived, my brother and I ran to the kitchen to see if Aunt Anna would sneak us a taste of the gravy. My mother used to dip a piece of Italian bread in the pot of gravy and let us put cheese on top and she called it her bread pizza. It was marvelous. My Aunt Anna brought us over to the table and proudly presented a huge platter of roasted chicken. My brother and I were expecting a pot of gravy, but instead we were flabbergasted and horrified to see the chicken heads and feet along with its other parts on the platter. My aunt was so excited to share this delicious entrée with us that she was totally unaware that we had never seen or eaten them before as we considered those parts inedible. Out of the corner of my eye, I caught my dad's eyes and instantly knew that we were to zip our lips, be polite and thank our aunt for such a wonderful dish. We didn't have to eat those parts but we had to show our respect for all of her effort and good intentions.

Circumstances and events of this caliber cause us to pause and analyze the situation so that we can choose our words appropriately and avoid embarrassment to to others. How do we know when to be silent? What determines the use of discretion or evasive maneuvers? Is there a risk of exposure to criticism, imposed judgment or ridicule? Is it worth the effort? How much information do we impart, full or partial disclosure?

All these questions swirling around in our heads demanding correct timing, resolution and closure from us with no easy solution or formula except courage and strength of character.

"Speak when spoken to." "Discretion is the better part of valor." "Tread lightly." "Think before you act." Old clichés but very pertinent to resurrect in our thoughts, reminding us of those who were before us. Theologians, philosophers and historians witnessed and experienced similar situations; their teachings encouraging us to be open-minded, to seek, find and voice the truth by example following and applying the lessons learned from their mistakes, failures and triumphs.

Speaking or silence—an uncomfortable dilemma all in the order of things; a part of everyday life. Deal with it or not, the choice is self-owned, personal, non negotiable and private. Stand up and be counted or cower in silence; the facts and alternatives have been presented, pick one.

To speak or not to speak—six words packing a great deal of weight, meaning, intent and consequence. They are associated with situations requiring answers, remarks and statements to sensitive, touchy questions concerning various categories and topics.

For example seeking an opinion of a personal nature, personality or appearance places the person in an awkward position pondering over either negative or positive responses.

Proprietary knowledge concerning the job and workplace that requires legal guidance before answering.

Unconscionable information involving marital status and relationships, fidelity, finances of friends and family testing issues of conscience, integrity and morality.

Serious medical information and decisions of a family member bearing ethical, religious and moral virtues burdened with sole responsibility for an individual's healthcare.

Financial disclosures, lifestyle and security information necessary for references or employment concerning friend, family, neighbors and co-workers, requested from official organizations investigating background checks.

All the above carry a heavy price tag, placing us in a questionable, legal, moral and religious dilemma, and forcing us to examine our conscience, test our logic, and challenge our opinions and thoughts. There are no written rules, timesheets, or guidelines associated with this state of affairs. Factual knowledge, experience and wisdom are the tools needed to analyze, dissect and evaluate the situation; but in the end, the answer often originates from intuition, gut feelings and common sense, all in combination with sound reason formulating the decision. The Catholic teaching advises us to stand firm in our beliefs but to agree to disagree and maintain our relationship, affection and friendship for one another.

EQUAL OPPORTUNITY

Nice thought often just words.

I wonder who determines equality. What are the rules, guidelines and qualifications that determine sameness? As a matter of fact, how do we know if they are equal?

I recently sat through a review of my job performance. I have been judged and qualified as satisfactory. What data was reviewed to arrive at this determination? Was I measured by criteria pertinent to my experience and type of work? Was the reviewer knowledgeable of my work habits, skill, speed and accuracy in the actual task assigned? All these questions have been spinning out of control in my mind since I read the paperwork reviewing my work habits and capability. Since I have been categorized as satisfactory under the guise of smooth words and polished sentences resulting in a very small insulting increase in pay, I feel disappointed, cheated and judged without just cause. "How do I rectify satisfactory and move forward to above satisfactory," I asked? The answer was vague at best.

Our work ethics, personality and IQ are exposed, probed, dissected and predetermined in writing to be digested, absorbed, put to memory and signed within a minimal response time. The reviewee has very little time to recall past events or situations that may have contributed to the statements of fact recorded on paper.

Regardless of who is right or wrong the outcome is standard, the same. Opposition and questions are voiced, heard in sympathy with a practiced façade of remorse, role play and shared experience. The document is signed and a sigh of relief is gasped ending an uncomfortable scenario on both sides setting the stage for the next person.

Has the person received an honest and true recitation of their worth and contribution to an employer? Is the reviewer a responsible upright fair person without influence, malice or condition? In my situation the person who wrote the review had no interface with me or the work I do. He was a supervisor of another department asked to do the review because my manager left the company and there wasn't anyone for this task.

Only the individual can truly know the worth of their performance and answer the question of whether he or she has been honestly represented.

Is it equal opportunity or managerial power and position overshadowing true vision and fairness?

Enough is Enough

Recently my cousin and I were engaged in one of our many serious intellectual conversations or shall I say debate. She spoke I listened, I spoke and she listened, both processing and digesting the information presented. We are very tuned into each other's nuances and reactions observing any changes in one another's posture. So I wasn't at all surprised to hear her say, "What is it? What is wrong?" I anticipated her questions but was finding it difficult to explain what was taking place in my brain at that time.

Annoyance, frustration, anger, boredom bombarding my thoughts like rapid gunfire one right after the other, fighting for space to dig in and remain causing me to respond with half-hearted and vague responses to her questions. In our best interest, we chose a neutral subject, relieved the tension, lightened the mood, returning calm and laughter in the atmosphere.

When all were asleep, I reflected on the activities of the day especially "the conversa-tion", as it was very disconcerting for me to react to many different feelings hitting so quickly leaving me at a loss as to how to organize and deal without interrupting the flow of conversation nor control the physical signs my body was portraying.

Are there times when some information is too disturbing to handle? Do we have a need to know all these facts when there is very little we can do to change things beyond our control? Do the subject matters importance and impact outweigh our distaste and desire not to know?

Politics, religion, opinions are precarious volatile topics designed to stimulate and cause reactions on a scale ranging from mild annoyance to, in some cases, actual violence. When do we draw the line, cut the cord and end the flow speech before it erupts into a danger zone? How do we end our participation in the discussion without conveying the wrong impression, changing the mood or appearing rude?

At my age I often lose or forget my train of thought and find myself interrupting the speaker so that I can get it out before it leaves me for places unknown. This faux pas is immediately followed by my sincere and embarrassed apology. It is a little scary and sad about this occurrence, but it is part of my aging process, so I must deal with it the best way possible for me. Since this is a recent affliction, I was not aware that a large percentage of the population of my age or older experience the same situation making me consciously aware of the camouflage and signs of others who interrupt me for the same reason. In my conversations with friends and family, we make a joke, call it a senior moment and continue the conversation without unkind notice or pause. With all of this said, I have found a plausible response and solution for interrupting and changing the subject in conversations with serious and stressful undertones guaranteed to send my brain into overload.

I speak, they listen, they speak, I interrupt and change the subject. Oops, Sorry.

Please Don't Go There

Sometimes facts bluntly stated are more than we wish or need to know. Our experience, personalities and IQ determine how much information is warranted in order for us to get the point. My mind instantly visualizes the info sending me pictures that range from weird to down right scary causing nasty side effects.

Situations providing too much knowledge cause my personality, emotions and thoughts to run amuck, my mind adding or deleting images from the chaos. Not pleasant by any stretch, definitely something I need not experience since my mind is naturally busy on its own.

It seems to me to be a matter of timing when instinct and intuition help us to curtail the out- pouring of certain facts and details. If the state of mind is alert and on guard, we have an edge on the timing allowing us to prevent the flow of words thereby preventing fall out. More often this ideal situation is non-existent capturing the mind's attention at a busy moment subjecting it to the full onslaught of the story, unable to stop the flood of words and pictures formulating in the brain.

Whether we like it or not, good or bad, weird or scary, it strikes seizing the opportunity to unload and dump. Loudly saying those magic words, "Please don't go there" only works when uttered at the precise moment when the speaker hesitates and is in the process of taking that little breath. If heard at the right time they may offer us a respite and block and censure their dissertation. In the event of failure, there are other options a bit silly but worth a try. Covering your ears, singing and walking away – are they effective? Probably not, because if the speaker is determined to invade and bombard our minds with a barrage of useless, superfluous information, sooner or later they will hit their target.

"Don't go there." Ah, what the hay, go for broke and take the ride. Worse things have happened after all "pain builds character"

That old adage rings true, "Fewer words are better spoken," not in this scenario.

A Right To Know

During one of many reflective moments my thoughts break away from the task at hand pondering over things that weigh heavy on my mind. This brainstorming episode is sparked by current or passed events that haven't been resolved in my head.

On this particular occasion I am troubled by the lack of recognition, understanding and appreciation for the age and ability of the elder generation within my space and time. I fail to understand how family and friends can request strenuous, laborious jobs under the guise as favors that are well beyond the physical limits and capabilities of the person.

Occasionally, parents are requested by their children to baby sit, house clean, garden or other sundry tasks in order to help out in a pinch providing both parties with a sense of satisfaction, good feeling, bonding and pride. A healthy environment is formulated providing a sense of belonging, need, usefulness and youth in addition to contentment and gratification. They become active participants with the family working together for the common good able to schedule their time in accordance with their activities and agenda.

Those who take advantage of the older generation by selfishly disregarding the stability and health of their elder parents and relatives trigger my gripe. They endanger them exposing them to health and safety issues in order to satisfy their own needs. Out of greed, stupidity, material things, they think of themselves first without consideration for anyone or thing placing older family members in an uncomfortable, awkward position leaving them no recourse, option or choice.

As the body declines, the ability to perform physical arduous tasks diminishes, limiting the amount of work hours, stamina and strength required to complete the job, causing stress and strain, stretching it beyond its capability or worse.

What do they do? How do the older people say no? How can they relay the message to those who thoughtlessly request favors beyond their boundary?

Their pride and independence challenges their reasoning and prejudices their negative response causing them anxiety and trepidation. They accept the responsibility placing their joints and stamina in jeopardy, possibly suffering untold ramifications and consequences afterward.

The aging process is precarious at best, natural changes occurring in body chemistry, shape, physical composition and endurance. Mental, social and outward appearance are signs of its effect in conjunction with apprehension, fear and anxiety of the unknown. All factors considered, reasonable thought is needed, not required, before asking for one's service.

Many everyday jobs appear harmless on the surface unbeknownst to us, but seen through the eyes of an older person they can be daunting.

There is a percentage of people who age well, fit as fiddles healthy models for AARP ads, and able to leap tall buildings without breaking a sweat; but in the real world, the majority are experiencing changes in lifestyle, an easier place, a slowing down, setting aside the hustle and bustle with less stress and strain, hopefully in anticipation of their new way of life.

They have earned the right to enjoy, to plan their own activities, agenda, time and space to determine their individual limits and guidelines. They have served their time and as the saying goes, "They have been there, done that."

It is time for the younger generation to take up the gauntlet, carry the torch and walk the talk allowing the older members of society moments of joy and happiness, their day in the sun. In recognition for their experience, knowledge, loving care and unquestionable service, they deserve our utmost respect, appreciation, admiration and consideration. Their memories are indelible imprints stored in our minds and hearts, timeless and unforgettable, earning them the right to say no.

No Time

It was quiet, too quiet. The silence was haunting, unnerving the bullet swooshing through the air silent but lethal. They sensed the danger but are too late. They never heard the bullet coming; the end was quick. No time to envision the faces of their loved ones to verbalize their love, say goodbye or offer a prayer before meeting their Maker.

On the other side of the hill, the soldiers were settled in for the night whispering small talk unaware of the fate of their comrades. The enemy pulled the trigger sending deadly bullets their way fast and furious. They heard the sound, knew what was coming. They scrambled into action firing back defending their country and protecting each other. The bullets kept coming, no time to check on one another. They knew it was their time. Someone or all would not make it. Those critically wounded were lifted out to the helicopters waiting to be airlifted to a medical facility. They were on borrowed time. Were they able to share their heart, that final breath of love, and send it traveling on the wind to those they love and hold dear? Did they make restitution in preparation to fulfill their destiny?

Everyday the men and women of the military are exposed to atrocities and horror way beyond our imagination. Their bodies are being maimed and mutilated; their lives changed forever. All their hopes and dreams destroyed, vanished in an instant.

Why does this have to be? Perhaps we should take a look back in to the time when the leaders of the tribes and kingdoms took up the gauntlet and lead their warriors into battle? What if the leaders and politicians of the world would "talk the talk" and lead the troops into the war they decided to declare? Would their hands-on experience open their minds and hearts to an alternative means of resolution, offer a different perspective, perhaps second or third thoughts before subjecting humanity to the carnage and death of war?

Today's philosophy and way of living has shifted us to dedicate our energy toward ourselves, greed, opportunity and advancement. "What is in it for me?" has become the mentality of today. Our lives are on speed control, too busy for connecting and bonding with each other. Our time and priorities are given sparingly and taken away replaced by some excuse, they are a commodity bought and sold depending on the market value, time and place. Our love and relationship with family and friends is constantly being tested. We are at the risk of losing a precious, valuable and loving gift never to be captured or retrieved again. Once jeopardized, it is never the same.

Will we hear the bullet coming?

Will we have the chance to right the wrong, to say we are sorry, to fix the hurt we caused? Will we be able to recapture the emotions and feelings that were lost in the mix? Can we re-establish the connection and cement the bond with those we neglected?

FATE

A gleam in their eye, a happy thought

Creation, birth the cycle begins

Embryo, child, adolescence, adult

Free will, decisions, choices

No interference, pressure or force

God's plan, His way

Trials, tribulations, joy and sorrow

Disappointment, lucky, penalties or rewards

Sickness, health, fortune, poverty

Life and death, heaven and hell

Destiny unknown, undetermined, in God's hands.

Fate!

The World Has Changed

In light of the moral and ethnic challenges facing us today, my mind envisions a similarity between the cause and effect of the biblical story of Noah's Ark, the war, flood and disasters of ancient times repeating history occurring in the world today.

Growing up in a religious environment, I was taught right from wrong, kindness to others and integrity and honesty. The concept of sin influenced my judgment and decisions. Greed, lying, immorality, stealing, divorce and adultery forbidden by the Ten Commandments were mortal sins, unacceptable behavior, punishable intolerable behavior depending on the severity either by civil law or common law.

Today divorce, gay marriage, sex out of wedlock, abortion, adultery the list goes on, is tolerated and accepted as the norm. People today have no moral issue with these wrongs. The future generations are growing up with a nonchalant attitude concerning this immoral way of life. The code and rules of measuring such behavior has shifted tilting the scales toward leniency and tolerance. Under the guise of individual rights, children and adults are justifying unacceptable inappropriate absolutely wrong behavior.

God gave us free will to make choices and fulfill our individual destiny armed with faith in our beliefs, confidence and hope in ourselves and love for our fellowman.

How and when did things go wrong? Where is the morality, fellowship and spirituality in people? Does it still exist or is it buried deep down unreachable?

What has happened to the world? War, floods, abuse in the church, corruption in government, greed etc. have crept in replacing kindness, honesty and integrity. The war in Iraq is responsible for the death of many young men and women with no solution in sight. Flooding in areas causing havoc, death and illness due to greed and inept political representative.

Priests accused of abusing children under the semblance of church and religion.

Corruption in business and finance involving political representatives and corporate leaders.

Greed in overcharging and gouging prices for goods in order to make money.

Removing the word God from the Pledge of Allegiance and civil government documents.

How does God see this? His creation to His image and likeness destroying and corrupting His world. Children soon to be adults growing up in an unsafe, immoral environment without belief in a Supreme Being.

Those who remained faithful have faded into the background quiet and silent horrified over the transformation, but inactively unresponsive and unmotivated to promote change. Where do we go from here? How much worse can it get?

Inhumanity has replaced our humanity. The divinity of the church and spirituality of the faithful have been compromised.

We must overcome fear, voice our thoughts, express our feelings and place our trust in God seeking His help and guidance to rise again powerful and strong.

"Wisdom to the wise and knowledge to those who understand."

Daniel 2:21

CHAPTER 10

The Golden Years

Our life cycle begins in the womb, Birth, infancy, childhood, adolescence, adulthood, are all as advancing steps within the growing process. We are either climbing up or falling down we experience peaks and valleys. Struggling to weather life's hurdles; our endurance is challenged and our trust tested.

Our health is precarious. Pain, sorrow, happiness and joy are obstacles to be faced defined and conquered. Our finances are defined set aside for retirement.and must be reviewed and conserved trips and vacations delayed or cancelled subject to many uncontrollable variables.

It is a time of passing a change our retirement promising anticipation of carefree activities devoid of stress and overwhelming responsibilities. It is a time to relax and kick back as we recapture memories and events. It is a time for reliving and revisiting them with mature eyes and sensibility, contemplating the messages our youth may have missed. We are scheduling, planning and marching to our individual beat without constraint or censure. Ideal as it sounds, the dream has flaws. Many factors affect its physical shape; attitude and spirit all must be in alignment healthy and strong. Our minds ascend and our bodies tire, showing the wear and tear of abuse and hard work throughout the years. Some age gracefully, spirit and body healthy and active, while others decline. The body deteriorating slowly day by day, its warranty in jeopardy.

Our goals accomplished, we set out to enjoy the fruits of our labor, although physically challenged.

Mileage accrued traveling from doctor to doctor, one for each ailment, testing, probing keeping the body tuned up, greased and oiled; pills for this and pills for that. Our good days are filled with enjoyment and pleasure; the bad confined, resting, thankful for the good ones.

Here are some words of wisdom I've picked up along the way:

1. When waking up in the morning, allow a half hour for checking
    a. what part of the anatomy hurts, creaks or clacks
    b. take the necessary pills and plan your day.
2. If you wake up everyday with pain, you know you are old.
3. Thank God for everyday you can open your eyes and see the dawn.
4. Loud and mysterious body sounds, are indicative of ingestion/digestion in motion. Keep GasX maximum strength, gallon size at the ready.
5. Gravity, a woman's downfall. Body parts shifting and changing in complete fall out.
6. Viagra a vanity pill uplifting for men.
7. Herbal teas infused memory enhancement, a required drink.
8. Tylenol on hand to kill the pain.

The list is endless, but you get the picture. The Golden Years, they suck!!!

CHANGE

Events, circumstances, different, unavoidable

Medical, physical, social, mental

Tests, scans, results, life altering

Sickness, disease, illness, physiological

Debilitating, dysfunctional, painful, mind-effected

Walking, standing, talking, lifestyle redefined

Incapacitated.

Blink of an eye, snap of the fingers, in an instant

Dependence, motion, confidence lessened

Stamina, agility, ability stolen, taken away

Capacity, understanding, diminished, below the norm

Communication, speech, lowered, incoherent

Assistance, help, support required, a necessity

Mental outlook, self worth, reduced, changed

Life's cycle, journey, destiny, fate

Geriatric change.

SENIOR MOMENT

During one time or another, every one of us has experienced a momentary forgetfulness a lapse in memory camouflaged by the usual excuses and clichés.

"Oops I forgot" uttered many times in haste and hurry said to oneself during inopportune times. For example, while in the supermarket discovering something missing from the shopping list as we stand in the check out line and experience instant recollection, we race down the aisle, retrieve it and place it in the cart, the incident quickly set aside.

Response time: seconds/minutes.

"Hello where have you been?" absent-mindedness—a blank moment while standing in the pantry oblivious to the cause and the object needed from the shelves. Searching its contents for a vision, back tracking our steps hoping for a sign to trigger its identity. At times our momentum and train of thought is briefly interrupted; we feel dazed and stare into space questioning time wondering about the where, when, why of what we were doing.

Response time: minutes.

"Oh sorry, what did you say?" blank stare—preoccupied while focusing on other things we are unaware of our surroundings, voices fading into the background, a temporary departure from the present. A simple jolt or noise nudges us back into the flow of conversation rejoining the party with "hum, yes, oh, ah, that is true" clueless as to what was being said.

Response time: minutes possible one-half hour.

"Sorry, I am having a senior moment"—a personification/combination of all the above experienced by those of us reaching maturity entering the so-called golden years. Whenever an idea strikes, we must instantly voice it or write it down less it take flight and disappear in the wind.

While conversing with friends or family a question or comment escapes us; in frustration we continue speaking frantically searching our memory banks only to confess those truthful words "I had something to tell you, but I forgot".

All of us have been in similar circumstances, used the standard retorts in explanation for frequent periods of forgetfulness, failure to recall times past and present, loss of one's train of thought challenging our brain to remember.

Response time: a variable.

In desperation we break out the memory enhancement remedies vowing to faithfully ingest on a daily basis.

Awareness dawns an acceptance, and respect for our age is realized. As part of the aging process, we move on armed with confidence, assurance, humor, healthy attitude and disposition for life's challenges and changes.

With our head held high, best foot forward aided by walker or cane, slowly but surely with God's help, we strive to do our best facing present and future Senior Moments.

GAINING WEIGHT

Scale tips, needle slides back and forth, the number flashes

Eyes blink once, twice and then again finally focused.

Stunned in shock, like a deer captured by the headlights of a car, the number registers.

A loud scream echoing in our mind bursting through our lips.

Disbelief, inaccuracy, it needs repair. That is the cause not the carbs, sweets or snacks; they were just a few perhaps a trifle more.

Walk away don't look back, all excuses tired and used.

The mirror waits, it doesn't lie or distort the image—bulges and pounds visible not pretty, unattractive.

Face the facts, make the promise, dust off the books, turn the pages and begin the fast and deprivation. Move forward exercise, diet and behave—turn on the willpower, drudge up the determination—the road is long the ritual has begun.

We eat a little something sinful just to get the body started, armed and ready.

Not too big, not too small, a cup of this, a cup of that.

Satisfied our conscience appeased our mood has changed, the pace is set, motivation high.

Reality accepted we face the music and pick up the tune to start the dance for tomorrow is another day!!

THE MAKEOVER

This old chassis could use a good makeover. The parts need a good refurbishing and vitalization.

A grease job to lubricate my joints to "walk the talk".

An oil change to lower my cholesterol count to improve a caring and sympatric heart.

A system flushing for my digestive track, a promise to provide healthy eating for myself and loved ones.

A coolant check, an application of anti-freeze for my hot flashes for me to remain calm in times of crisis.

A diagnostic scan of my internal clock, quick response and mobility, so that I will be there for those who need me.

An interior detailing of mind, senses and attitude to forgive and forget the wrongs that have been done to me.

Exterior detailing of skin and hair. Nails buffed, simonized and polished. Ointment, salves and balm applied to scratches, nicks and dents to heal old scars left behind.

Spare tires exercised, toned and firmed; in theory, realistically supported with the purchase of good under garments, a vanity level check.

New paint job to dump those old cosmetics that have been sitting around for decades to seek advice on new ways of use and application. Review use of over-the-counter medications to seek alternative and natural remedies.

Take inventory of my wardrobe. Stodgy, boring old fashion clothes thrown out, replaced with classic, stylish, sexy are in but not too sexy; can't get too crazy. It would be too shocking to my hormones and libido. My husband would have to consider Viagra. I am digressing; all this talk is stimulating my hot flashes. Hugging, cuddling, touching and feeling appreciated, satisfying offering spiritual contentment superseding physical pleasures.

Refuel my tank with low octane gas, use Beano and cut back to regular strength Gas X to change habits of eating and drinking and focus on moderation.

Adjust the brakes and steering column to curb my anger and short temper, to steer my mind to stop and think before reacting.

New glasses to see and understand the changing times; new wipers to wipe away old prejudices, archaic notions and beliefs; dark lenses to shade the eyes from seeing too much.

Check gums, mouth and teeth to speak up, voice the truth and share words and ideas against unfair laws and practices.

The chassis has been overhauled, the transition complete. The door is open, the gear is in drive, my destination determined. The system navigator (God) is mapping the way. My journey has begun. There is no turning back, my destiny is in motion.

I am out of the box. My words are for hire; my opinions, food for thought. Watch out baby!!

Now That You're Home

Why is it that those who are not retired share the misconception that because retirees are not officially employed they have nothing to do with their time? They feel compelled to provide us with ideas, options and opinions on how we can utilize and occupy our days. They instinctively jump to the wrong conclusion, assume the wrong idea and utter comments over and over, "Now that you have the time" or "Now that you are home".

As a newly retired person, correction a newly early (63 year old) retiree, I seem to be the recipient of these pre-disposed canned remarks although I understand they bear me no malice and just want to be helpful. For example, the other day I met a friend at our local library. After we exchanged the usual greetings, she proceeded to give me a tour of the area commenting on the various books offering suggestions on this and that, making recommendations on which books I should read. Suddenly I could feel the hairs on the back of my neck standing on end for I knew it was coming and I had to brace myself, purse my lips and fasten my face as not to reveal my reaction. Her mouth opened lips at the ready her assumption in place reverberating, "Now that you have the time" "Sign out two or three of them" and take home some DVDs; they will help you pass the time.

I must admit I envied those who were retired simply because I wanted the freedom and opportunity to do all the things on my newly titled "kick the bucket list". It never occurred to me that retirement meant nothing to do; in fact it was just the opposite.

My days are so occupied it is hard to believe I managed to squeeze in the time to go to work. It seems that the time whizzes by in the blink of an eye.

My husband and I are early risers who are creatures of habit. He begins his day digesting and reading the paper, breakfast and internet surfing. I on the other hand am committed to a healthy schedule of morning prayer and a fifty-minute exercise program.

My husband has been enjoying his retirement for over ten years and fills his day satisfying his passion for crafts, puzzles, exercise and golf. His weekly schedule also includes lunch with the boys, catching up on the news and planning their golf rounds and outings. Since I have become part of the mix, we agreed our retirement was a joint venture that would include time together and time apart. Before rising from bed we review our schedule for the day. Lunch with friends is planned on the same day allowing us to enjoy a separate time out. Later in the evening we catch up and share the events of the day. Our personal activities occupy our time performing household chores, shopping, an occasional outing followed by lunch or dinner depending on the length of our trip, home and relaxation.

The afternoon hours before dinner are our personal free time to do our thing. For me it is writing, reading a book, meditating, putzing around the kitchen trying new recipes or just taking a nap. My husband plays on the computer, reads his favorite magazine, watches TV and catches up on his favorite sports. We have booked several trips for when the weather breaks to satisfy and enjoy my love of the ocean and his love for golf. Although I am not a golfer, I act as his caddy offering praise and awe while enjoying the beautiful scenery and exercise at the same time.

Following several decades of work and sacrifice, we share financial security and a nice home. God has given us a good marriage, stable health and a chance to enjoy our lives together. We are truly blessed and thankful to Him.

The assumptions and concepts that retirees spend their days inactive without ways of spending their time is an incorrect misnomer. It is not "Now that you have time", but "Can you spare the time"?

THE UMBRELLA

It is a clear crisp day. You are sitting at your desk absorbed in concentration when suddenly without warning a loud noise rings followed by total darkness. The sudden change in surroundings promotes a feeling of fear and anxiety. The generator returns a minimal amount of light, your co-workers begin to react changing the mood of the room; their voices and camaraderie release the tension changing emotions. Outside the weather has turned ugly. Wind, cold and rain have knocked out the power. The loud speaker relays the message for everyone to leave the building due to a total power outage of the entire area. Facilities and computers will be inoperable for several hours. The words are bittersweet affording a free day, but at the moment you must take precaution and deal with the outside obstacles. Searching for a means of protection, you find an umbrella in the desk drawer. Armed and ready you venture outside.

The umbrella is composed of steel, has a sturdy foundation, consistently able to hold up against the storm helping to minimize our exposure to the wind and rain. Its design and character offer stability, insurance and protection whenever its service is demanded. We maintain it keeping it close at hand and rely upon it in the event of a change in the weather.

The day begins as usual. Routine chores and scheduled plans await completion when suddenly you notice a change overpowering your body. Your first reaction is bewilderment wondering what is happening, the fear and anxiety ready to surface. You realize these changes are taking place at a rapid pace and you must seek help. Without warning, your life and the world around you has changed.

Many of us, especially the elderly, experience sudden changes causing a decline in the condition and state of their mental and physical health. Nature's aging process challenging, attacking the body slowing down its functions, taking away its stamina and endurance, causing anxiety, fear and terror in the elderly. They are forced to seek help grabbing onto something, someone to help alleviate their symptoms, protect, shelter, love and care for them. Having no choice, they are forced to hand over the health, welfare, decision-making and total care of their person. They trust that the caregiver, their umbrella will do the right thing, make the right decisions and stay the course. Someone who is strong, patient, caring and loving, willing to endure, commit, and companion their loved one toward their final journey.

Who will it be; the daughter, son, family member, relative or close friend? The challenges ahead are daunting, testing human endurance and patience.

Taking emotions on a roller coaster ride laughing and joyous one day crying and sad the other, never sure when and if the time is near.

It is a road no one chooses to travel. Unfortunately when the time comes, we will all go there. The traveler experiences the pain, suffering, its highs and lows each day flowing into the next; time, the enemy ravaging and causing loss of one's abilities. They begin to realize God's will, communicate with Him through prayer, faith, belief and communion, all methods offering acceptance and calm to the inevitable.

The caregiver, just as the umbrella, is dedicated, steadfast, tenacious, soothing, loving, caring someone who motivates, calms, relieves the fear and anxiety providing shelter, comfort and hope from nature's wrath.

Both parties taking the journey, one reaching the final resting place fulfilling their destiny going home to Paradise and seeing their Creator, while the other is filled with questions, many questions with no answers visualizing their own vulnerability causing, fear and apprehension subjecting them to experience and knowledge beyond their control or choice to know. What path will their journey take? Who will be their umbrella? Memories good and bad haunting them of the trials and challenges they faced, reminders of what may or will be for them when roles are reversed.

"Time heals all wounds." "It is in God's hands." "Life goes on." Sayings applied in times of need, a strong sturdy umbrella surrounding us minimizing the hurt and pain helping to relieve a troubled soul, and soothe a broken heart, enabling us to weather the storm. Faith in the God who is the caretaker, our spiritual umbrella.

SLEEP

Winter, summer, spring or fall

Morning, noon or night

Sitting in a chair, watching TV, reading a book

Futon, sofa, couch, recliner or chair

Relaxing, lackadaisical, resting, dozing

Wrapped snuggled in a sheet or blanket safe and warm

Sounds of the night, fading in the distance

Sheep jumping, climbing over a fence, counting, counting

Hot chocolate, milk or tea remedies tried and true

Head nodding, eyes drooping, partly closed, almost shut

Half in, half out, a dreaming state

Take five, snooze, zz's, forty winks, nap

Dreams or nightmares

The cadence of life

Shut lights

Close eyes

Rest, relax

Calm, peaceful

A dreaming state or not

Sleep!

"Acting silly and carefree is so much fun."

CHAPTER 11

THE LIGHTER SIDE OF THINGS

The introduction to this chapter presents a challenge because I am at a loss as to how to title, explain and justify its contents. The poems were written on the spur of the moment, perhaps in a silly mood or a creative whim. I am not sure of the how or why of it, but the topics are simple without serious energy, thought or connotations.

I have decided to take a sample of the contents and express my feelings and memories as I reread them. "The Mustache" reminds me of my father's uncle who was visiting us from Italy. I was only five years old but I have a very vivid picture of it in my mind. It was a handle-bar mustache, and of course, I didn't know its name, but I knew it was very funny to look at and it wiggled a lot when he spoke. He used to stand in front of the mirror and put wax on the ends and twirl one side and then the other. I used to wonder how it felt when he ate his food. Did it get in the way or did it get wet when he drank liquids?

As I was flipping the channels on the TV, I happened to catch a show on Oprah that caught my attention. They were discussing toilet paper. It seems they had polled the audience to determine which direction the toilet paper sheets rolled out. The majority of them, including Oprah, preferred the toilet paper to point downward toward to the floor because it facilitated the roll and was easy to tear. Thus, the poem "Carta di Bagna."

The wind reminded me of the eerie sounds of the air creeping through the windows in a scary movie. Our house is on the top of a hill and is opened on all sides, leaving it exposed to the full force of the elements. When the wind blows, the hanging plants and furniture sway back and forth, rearranging their postions. As I stood watching the dance of the wind, I was inspired to write the poem "The Mighty Winds."

We all experience days when we focus on the lighter side of things, giving ourselves a reprieve from serious thoughts and concerns. It feels good to just enjoy the mundane, and if the mood strikes, act a little silly. I don't get many days like this and am delighted I took the time to write down some of those moments.

THE MIGHTY WINDS

Trees bending, branches strained
Leaves whirling toward the sky
Objects rolling round and round,
Here and there, everywhere.

Whistling, eerie, creaking, ghostly sounds
of houses groaning and swaying,
Trashcan lids flying,
Bouncing across streets and lawns.

Cars swaying, slightly shaking,
Wind whistling through the windows,
Lights flickering with wires and tree limbs downed.
Flags waving stretched straight forward on their poles.

Wind chimes dancing playing their tune.
Flowers losing their petals, falling limbs bending
Shutters banging, curtains blowing
Windows whistling creating scary sounds and noises.

Hats and umbrellas lost in the breeze seeking new owners;
Hair eschew, all every which way, blowing unencumbered.

Nose running, chest pounding and breath catching
God's mighty breath, nature's angry force.

The Mighty Winds

THE MUSTACHE

Above the lip, under the chin, a fuzzy mass

Brown, black, red, blonde or gray

Bristles, hairs, coarse, wiry or soft

Partial, middle, full, odd shaped or contoured

Curly, straight, twisted, crooked, natural or dyed

Upward or downward

Waxed, slick or jelled

Good looking, handsome, ugly, mediocre, eh!

Handsome, debonair, distinguished, just for men

Lotions, creams, concoctions, remedies/tricks of disguise

Removed, tweezed, pulled, unwanted, a women's albatross

Branded with milk, white or chocolate.

The Mustache

Chock Ski

Small, medium, large, extra large, gigantic

Wood, plastic, plaster or steel

Colorful, frightful, vibrant or dull

Ugly, smart, tasteful, awful or in vogue

Souvenir, keepsake, ornament, gift, bric-brac, or junk

Exciting, full of surprise, fun to receive

Laughter, happy, oops, ugh, oh my or ah

Birthday, Anniversary, Graduation, Thinking of You or just because

Displayed, cherished, stored away, recycled, or trashed

Whatever the season, time or place, occasion or not

Purpose, rhyme, reason or cause, sensible or funny

No matter the object, item or thing

The day is brightened, our step lighter and our heart full

What counts are the caring, feeling and thought

A chock ski is a chock ski.

CARTE DI BAGNA

Nature calls, we respond

Leaves, stones, cobs, grass, newspaper cut into pieces

Indoors, outdoors, outhouse, in the house

Woods, by the road, facility, in the can or john

On a roll, in a box, continuous or cut

Quilted or plain, Charmin, Scott, Cottonelle

Soft, fluffy, white, smooth or scratchy

Necessity, a must, required, natural, clean

Used, replaced, used, replaced mustn't run out

Round and round, over or under

Never ending, rolling, rolling.

Toilet Paper

RAIN

Clouds gathering, sky darkening, moisture forming nature's water

Condensation, evaporation, liquid dots rising and falling

Spritz, drizzle, buckets or deluge

Falling soft or hard, jewels of moisture pounding the surface

Thunder, lighting, wind, fog, cloudy and dark

Nature's fury, angry and proud

Scary, exciting, hair standing on end, skin wet

Senses awakened, alert and aroused

A rebirth, cleansing, regeneration of Earth, land and sea

Purification of mind, spirit and soul

Worries, inhibitions, stress and tears

Released, washed away, in preparation ready to begin anew

Relief, joy and happiness, cool and fresh

God's gift, the Rain.

BUGS

Webs, nests, hives, caves

Concrete, grass, woods, swamp

Indoors, or outdoors

Microscopic, tiny, small, medium or large

Furry, fuzzy, wiggled, squirmy

Bites, welts, bumps, bull's eye, lumps

Ugly, annoying disgusting, itchy, dirty

Critters, ants, bees, mosquitoes, wasps, ticks

Insects, moths, spiders, beetles

Infinite species, varieties, types and shapes

Bugs.

A Paintbrush

Bristles hairy, fuzzy and full, simple and sleek

Light or heavy, thick or thin

Attached to wood, stick or twig

Rolling, swirling, dipping swishing

In primary colors of every hue

Oils, watercolors, natural or mixed

Paper, canvas, other medium

Imitates, captures, portrays

Seeks essence, reality, substance

Finds the spirit, soul, beauty

An artist's extended hand, painted, directed, created

Animate, inanimate objects

People, places, animals, nature

The subject, immortalized, forever visible, remembered

Brought to life, remembered by a stroke of a brush

The Paintbrush

CRAYONS

A square box, 8, 24, 64 or more in number, an array of colors signifying God's handiwork and nature's bountiful gifts.

Various shades of green for the trees and grass, a habitat for animals and insects.

Blue and white for clouds and sky so bright the symbols of heaven's rewards.

Yellow for the sun, a large geometric icon caressing our bodies with its warmth and heat.

Multi-colors, orange, pink, etc. bright and cheerful gracing the flowers that spread joy and happiness throughout the world.

Red the color of Christ's blood shed for the sins of mankind.

Black for sadness and death, a time of remorse, consolation and grief.

Purple the color of penitence adorning the altar and worn by the priests in preparation of the holy days of the church.

Moods, emotions and energy changed and touched by color sparking and igniting the energy and power within.

Colors so beautiful and exotic capturing our voices speechless, impossible of description.

Crayons simple colored waxed sticks but oh so symbolic representing life, the world's canvas overloading our senses with infinitesimal sights and wonders extending their powers providing us with reasons to rise and shine and begin a new day.

PASTA

Short or long

Curly or straight

Rolled, folded, pressed or plain

Tubular or conical

Whole wheat, white, semolina, potato or cheese

Gnocchi, tortellini, fettuccine, all shapes and designs

Bought or homemade, naked or dressed

Cold or hot

Spaghetti, pasta, macaroni, no matter the name

Pasta rules

Pasta is king

Pasta is supreme!

LEFTOVERS

Gather ingredients, mix, smash, whisk

Pots, pans, or wok

Charcoal, gas or electric

Grill, roast, fry, or braise

High heat, low or simmer

Forks, spoons, knives

Plates large or small, round, square, or triangular

Garnish, arrange, place, fancy or plain

Chew, crunch, savor, tasty, and delicious

Wash, clean up, store, put away

Recycle, reheat, warm up, lukewarm, or cold

Camouflaged, changed, hidden, concealed, disguised

Casserole, pot pie, stir fry, pasta or salad

Once good, twice satisfactory, leftovers.

APPETIZERS

Small geometric culinary tidbits
Artistically styled and designed,
Tasty, tantalizing and fresh
Tempting the palate
Teasing the senses
Whetting the appetite with anticipation, joy and expectation.

Agents of conversation
Finger foods savory and delicious
Ingredients and composition exciting and mysterious
Simple or complex each morsel a single delight
Large or small, neat or sloppy
A surprise in every bite
Finger licking, lips smacking
Ohs and ahs all around

Starters or first course
Buffet or sit down
Fish meat, fowl and assorted veggies, a vegan's paradise
A superb beginning, middle or end
A pleasurable interlude satisfying and grand
Appetizers, hors d'oeuvres, or tapas an eating extravaganza!

BREAD

Yeast a primary ingredient active and bubbly

Sugar, flour, eggs and salt added for flavor

Rises, falls, rises again

Kneaded and shaped, all forms and sizes.

Loaves or rolls

Whole grain, wheat or rye

A staple in everyone's diet

A culinary delight.

The Lord's chosen vehicle

His Body our spiritual food

The miracle of the loaves and fishes feeding those who followed and believed

A religious symbol for holidays throughout the world

Blessed, revered and respected especially at Easter time.

Punched, pulled, stretched or twisted

However abused, it rises high, resilient and proud

A crusty exterior, a center soft, airy and light.

Bread! The food of life, a message for mankind.

This Bread is eaten once a year during the Easter holidays. I must admit that I have broken the tradition and made it again and again. It is delicious and reminds me of all the wonderful foods and activities of the season.

EASTER BREAD

Ingredients:
1 cup warm water
2 packages of yeast
1 ½ cups all-purpose flour
¾ cup shortening
1 cup granulated sugar
1 teaspoon salt
2 eggs unbeaten
1 egg white
4 teaspoons grated lemon rind
2 tablespoons anise seed
4 ½ cup all-purpose flour, sifted

Method of Preparation:
Combine the yeast and water together. Let stand for 5 to 10 minutes, enough to dissolve the yeast (1/2 cup). In a large bowl, place ½ cup of water and the sifted flour. Add the yeast to this mixture. Cover the bowl with a towel in a warm place for 2 hours. Combine the shortening, sugar and salt. Beat well and add 2 eggs and 1 egg white. Save the yolk to glaze the bread. Add 4 ½ to 4 ¾ cups of flour and anise seed to the shortening mixture and combine with yeast mixture. Work the dough with your hands until you get a soft dough. Let the bread raise overnight. In the morning braid the bread and raise again. Grease the pan and top the bread with egg yolk. Bake in a 350-degree oven for approximately 30 minutes. Once bread is cooled, make an icing and drizzle over top of bread.

To make the icing:
Ingredients:
2 cups 10X sugar
1 teaspoon lemon zest
Milk

Method of Preparation:
Combine sugar and lemon zest in a large bowl. Add milk gradually and mix until it forms a consistency thin enough to drizzle.

"This is a loving tribute to my family and friends."

CHAPTER 12

HEARTGIFTS

I tell this story exactly as it happened back in July, 2007 the day my mother passed away. My mother had a green thumb. She loved to grow plants, especially roses. She gave them tender care and would spend hours sitting on her porch watching their buds bloom and smelling their scent. When she became ill, the roses started to change. Just as her health declined, the rose leaves started to turn brown and they lost their fragrance. She would stumble outside to talk to them and try to treat them but her body was too weak. I tried to help but the roses did not respond to my attempts. I suggested we pull them out and replace them. My mother became very agitated and in a loud voice told me to leave them alone. She would take care of them as soon as she felt better. She never had that opportunity because God had different plans for her.

The funeral was over and everyone had gone home. Out of habit, I went down to her living quarters and stepped out onto her porch. Automatically my eyes focused on her rose bushes. They appeared dead. All the leaves had fallen off and the branches were dark and brittle. I made a mental note to pull them out as soon as possible. They looked the way I felt: tired and exhausted. Several days lapsed before I had time to tend to the business of the roses. As I approached the garden I was stunned to see that the leaves on the roses were vibrant green with several beautiful long stem roses on the branches. Tears were pouring down my face. I couldn't believe my eyes. I began speaking to my mother and told her she had kept her promise and brought those roses back to life. They are still very vibrant and healthy, a tribute to her loving care. Although our loved ones are gone, their life is merely changed, not ended, that those we love are still with us though unseen.

It had been two years since my mother's death, but whenever I go downstairs to her living area it does not feel abandoned or empty. It is as though her presence is still there. There have occasions when I have passed her bathroom and I can smell her bath soap as if she had just taken a bath. Before she died, I told how I couldn't bear to have her leave me that she had to come back and see me. I firmly believe that she has taken a different form and her spirit is working hand in hand with the angels to watch over us and pray for our health and safety.

Memory becomes your partner. It is a special gift God has given to us. We can recall it to remember our deceased loved ones, visualize their personality and the little nuances of their face and body. We can hear their voice, feel and share their prescence. We can picture the happy times we shared and relive the joy they gave us.

This chapter is a special tribute to my family and friends, without whom I would not be who I am. It is their enduring patience, love, caring and support that has carried me through life's events. Thank you are simple words but offered to them from the core of my heart.

THE GATHERING

A place warm and cozy welcoming its guests who will meet and visit together.

Grouped in bunches or alone observing others emerged in conversation each guest finding a comfortable niche.

Aromas of candles perfume the air creating a backdrop for the evening's festivities.

Foods are laden on a well-dressed table causing palates to salivate in anticipation of what's to come.

Music is playing in soft decibels, words in soothing tempos offering relaxation while recreating memories of times passed.

Couples dancing and swaying to their own beat sharing in the rhythm of the dance.

Wisps of conversation floating through the air happy, excited, private and sexy with promises of things to come.

Everyone partaking of a sumptuous repast consumed in an assortment of tastes, flavors and textures designed to arouse and satisfy all the senses.

A variety of beverages compliment a fabulous meal resulting in mellow feelings and relaxed motion.

Dessert, sweetly anticipated but quietly tucked in the background waiting its debut to climax this event. Artistically displayed is an array of sweet works of art and over the top concoctions created to make one swoon in ecstasy with temptations beyond control, a dramatic conclusion to a decadent indulgence.

With hearts full, stomachs content, good times spent, the evening is concluded with sounds of good-bye, safety stressed and God's blessing to all.

The McNellis Gathering

THANKSGIVING

Cars parked in the driveway, pumpkins, scarecrow and multi-colored mums welcome each guest.

Falling leaves, trees turning a chill in the air frost soon to come.

Savory aromas filled with spice perfuming the rooms teasing the senses.

A fire in the fireplace with burning embers sparkling bright and beautiful.

Candles glowing setting the atmosphere cozy and warm.

The table fully appointed showing a centerpiece of dried flowers and Tanya's paper turkey with crystal ornaments depicting the meaning and elegance of this special holiday.

Friends and family gathered around together sharing stories and recipes of nature's harvest.

Conversations flowing, voices humming and lips smacking in appreciation of the culinary repast enjoyed by all.

Dishes clanging, glasses tinkling, silverware ringing signaling the meal's end, a time to savor the moment and create new memories.

Sitting in front of the TV or cleaning up in the kitchen relaxed and content, all abound in joy and happiness.

Children sleeping in innocence their dreams sweet and happy.

Joy and love touching our hearts surrounding us with peace and gratitude for all the blessings bestowed on us this day.

A cameo picture, a moment in time to be remembered and cherished, a legacy passed on from generation to generation in years to come, a memory stored and cherished.

Thanksgiving at my house 2004!

FRIENDS

Special people whom God has chosen to cross our paths creating a spiritual bond, a physical connection with our mind and spirit.

Their very existence gives us joy, happiness and comfort.

Always at your side in times of sadness, heartache and tragedy, they are the voice of calm offering a shoulder to lean on and a helping hand through their actions and good deeds.

They are a powerful force behind you fighting in your corner lifting your spirits and motivating you beyond your limits cheering you forward.

They share your happiness holding your hand and smiling with you, two hearts joyous and fulfilled.

A presence felt whether near or far away offering support, wisdom, sound advice and understanding wherever/whenever needed.

Over the course of decades, they have stood the test of time at our sides on holidays, gatherings, special events, pain, illness and death.

Although busy with their own families and lives, they check in reminding us of their purpose and strength.

Although time has elapsed whenever we get together, we never tire of speaking or listening to each other absorbing one another's words, comfort and strength.

Thank God for His gift in creating such wondrous and unique spirits, someone I have the honor and privilege to call my friend.

One of A Kind

He is a loving person whose caring is truly dedicated to his wife and soul mate, Dot. Her disease (MS) suffered throughout these many years has rendered her incapacitated and dependent requiring 24/7 care and assistance.

A companion for life he pushes forward washing, feeding, carrying, motivating, nurturing and consoling, offering hope and love regardless of her condition and ability to communicate no matter how hard the course.

His own health in jeopardy, he endures, attacks and fights. His strength and energy driven from within his very being always helping, keeping her safe, alive and warm protecting regardless of the consequences to himself.

He has a no nonsense attitude, never giving up, defeat or surrender not a consideration or option.

He takes no credit, no bows, accolades or praise. It is his destiny, life's challenge. He feels privileged to perform for the time allotted by the Creator.

He is a rare and unique individual, a one of kind, a soul mate, our friend, Emil.

FAMILY DOCTOR

A large white house his office below, colorful decorations adorn the windows, entrance and door. An antique bench, coat hooks and a large scale appoint the foyer. Comfortable chairs, couch, fireplace and tables comprise the waiting room assuring the patient's comfort and ease. Magazines of every variety help to idle away the time shortening the wait. A candy dish filled with treats tempting and sweet. An occasional visit from Oliver, his pet dog greeting all with his bark begging for candy peppermints, his flavor of choice.

Files, paperwork, records and accounting handled efficiently, accurately organized, neatly arranged and respectively maintained. A professional, cheerful staff, upbeat, confident lending help and assistance to all offering a warm smile, a welcome environment, a caring and friendly experience.

His day begins at dawn visiting patients at the Hospital and Nursing Home offering consolation, comfort and well wishes to the sick and elderly of his flock. He is respected and revered by colleagues and staff. Wearing his white coat, stethoscope in his pocket, an aura competent, knowledgeable and wise; his skills, talent and expertise practiced for decades. Hundreds of patients throughout generations, some no longer here others patched up, mended, helped and cured all grateful and privileged to be under his care alive and well. Each patient treated as a friend greeted by name, recognized and remembered all part of his countenance. He inquires about job and family with sincere concern, guarding their immediate health and well being.

He patiently listens and absorbs our recantations, complaints, aches, pains, discomfort, trials and tribulations while performing a careful and thorough examination listening, probing, checking body reflexes, senses, creaks and noises in the joints. Wheels turning he studies and ponders the symptoms, the cause of the pain or ailment, details his diagnosis, prescribes current up-to-date treatment, methods, tests and prescriptions. Chats for a while, the patients are satisfied and relieved. His task accomplished, he continues treating and caring for his other patients. Breaking for lunch he returns phone calls, checks with the pharmacy, calms anxiety and sets things to order.

His patience, understanding, personality, caring spirit and kindness are dedicated in helping and healing his fellowman, his destiny fulfilled. A giant of a man, a wonderful human being, Dr. Battafarano.

Dr. O'Hara

A man of honesty, integrity and compassion, he travels the halls of Paoli Hospital making his rounds visiting his patients diagnosing their illness, healing sick hearts, calming fears and extending sincere care and advice.

He is a man determined and steadfast to his calling. His gift of knowledge, education and skill in the field of Cardiac Care has extended and saved the lives of many giving them a second chance and a better quality of life.

His friendly manner, pleasant disposition in conjunction with his high quality of learning, provide his patients with a feeling of hope relieving them of their anxiety and fear, making their office visit a good experience.

The office staff are quality personnel efficient and skilled in their field practicing respect and understanding toward all his patients. Records and files are organized and neatly filed, the confidentiality of each patient is protected; phone conversations are pleasantly handled quickly in order and with results.

Dr. O'Hara is a true champion focused on his patients fulfilling his destiny healing the sick. No one wishes illness on themselves, but it is a confident and secure feeling to know doctors like him who are true to their profession, qualified and in charge guarding over us.

Dr. O'Hara is a special doctor, understanding, dedicated to the health and wellness of his patients. My heartfelt prayers are offered in petition that God will watch over him, keep him healthy and strong, and help him to watch over us.

Good Men Are Hard to Find

I often wonder what forces of nature in the Cosmos or sign of the Zodiac collided and destined me to meet one William J. McNellis my husband, friend and confidant.

Raised by good Irish parents along with many siblings, he grew up schooled in good manners, common sense, an appreciation of financial security and a fine moral character.

Over the years we have had our good and bad times but we faced them together combining our virtues focusing on our determination of purpose, courage and strength.

Although there is a 13-year difference in our age, we share the same sense of rightness and morality although he posses a difference of opinion when it comes to finances; I possess a greater joy for spending than he.

He is a wonderful provider enabling us to live in a beautiful house and share a comfortable lifestyle. He has been supportive and patient toward my mother who lives with us. He is the buffer during the times my patience is tested and my nerves are strained beyond my limits.

I have never written down my feelings for him except in cards I give that are already versed. I can't explain why I am choosing this particular moment to put pen to paper, but I feel the need to honor the moment and say what is in my heart for this wonderful man.

Perhaps celebrating my 60th birthday is the motivation behind this catharsis. Whatever the reason, I am very blessed to have him as my friend, husband and companion to share my destiny and travel at my side down my life's journey.

Good Men are hard to find but luckily I found mine. Thank God for this blessing.

THE BIONIC MAN

Faster than a speeding bullet, more powerful than a locomotive—Not Exactly!

Gravity, age and circumstances of time challenge his endurance.

A bit slow and creaky, unsteady of step, he fights the battle of passing years.

Implants of a hip and knee assist him in starting the day enabling him to walk, run on the treadmill, play golf and climb stairs testing his bionic devices to the maximum.

His looks and physique appear younger than his 70 years with hair full, skin smooth.

With a heart and soul simple and honest, he accepts life's twists and turns with an upbeat, never-say-die attitude.

His manner is pleasant and congenial to all around him.

He possesses a treasure chest of knowledge and facts past and present waiting for dissertation upon request.

He loves machines and is fascinated by mechanical devices especially his power tools, computer and tractor.

He loves to tinker, create and craft things requiring patience and meticulous manipulation, his best tools being his hands.

His abilities and skills are boundless.

He is mister-fix-it. Anything that breaks he will take apart and spend hours digesting its working order and movements until he has mastered its complexity and fixed the problem.

Age has not slowed him down yet. Always active and alert, he keeps busy cutting grass and doing odd jobs around the house. The neighbors seek his advice in carpentry and plumbing—our garage and basement titled Bill's Home Depot.

Computer skills self-taught, he travels the website like a pro investigating news and events keeping his mind active and alert.

Who is this wonder of wonders able to reach beyond boundary?

Bill, the Bionic Man

The Quiet Man

Have you ever met someone who spoke volumes without uttering a single word?

A presence felt rather than seen.

He was an observer of his surroundings, people and their emotions.

He spoke softly, but his words carried wisdom and understanding leaving his listener with much to absorb and digest.

Time spent with him was precious and comforting almost as if you were wrapped in a warm blanket. You felt as though a burden was lifted from your very being.

His quiet manner and knowledge was a God given gift, that fortunately for the people who knew him, were able to experience in his lifetime.

He is truly missed but not forgotten.

Uncle Carmen, the Quiet Man.

Dear Amedeo,

Born of the same parents, you and I blood related, same genes, similar in looks, personality and temperament. Living with mom and dad sharing our Italian heritage customs, traditions, language and mannerisms.

Growing up together bonded in spirit and heart facing the good times and bad side by side courageous and strong. Encouraging one another's growth, motivation and determination, enjoying success together without jealousy, malice or resentment.

Although far away, we remain close talking on the phone, reminiscing old times and family news, exchanging holiday wishes, cards and letters. Visiting whenever possible, cherishing, savoring, appreciating the precious moments spent cooking, conversing, just enjoying each other's presence and comfort.

Over the years, harsh words, arguing, meanness or indifference has not passed between us. We have remained constant in our role as brother and sister practicing the rules, virtues, integrity and ethics taught and instilled in us by our parents.

Words can't express my feelings, emotions and gratitude for all we are, have been and will be. With you in my life always at my side, dependable and strong, I am complete, armed with your caring, love and support to handle whatever life offers.

My daily prayers ask God to keep you healthy and safe, for you are His precious gift to me, Joe, and I am privileged and proud to call you my brother.

Love,
Sofia

COMPUTER MAN

Mind alert, nerves of steel, swift reactions and dexterity

His nimble fingers weapons at the ready

Man vs. machine

Emails blocked

Blackened screen

No virus too complex

Inputs/responses too slow

Interfering bothersome spams

Man challenges, competes and spars

Bells and whistles sounding

Mouse clicking speedily burning rubber on its pad

Commanding/inputting messages

Man: eyes focused determined/strong

Machine: screen blinking, escaping capture

Back forth, back forth

Tension mounting

Machine chugging and groaning

Man waiting and smiling

Man Victorious!

Sharath, The Computer Man

Sweetie Kins

Pint size a reflection of her parents with thick raven black hair and shiny, mischievous chocolate brown eyes.

Plays with books, puzzles, colored balls and games.

Prefers to dress like a princess with sparkles, bangles and beads.

Loves the color pink in any fashion.

Smart as a whip with a mind older than her years.

She is talented, precocious, and loveable.

A whirlwind of motion, energetic, bouncy and sassy.

She enjoys birthdays, cupcakes and presents.

Her birthright is Indian, but she shows no boundaries.

Eats Indian, Italian and American foods—rice, pasta, pita and curry among her favorites.

She is a ray of sunshine on a cloudy day, a shining star in the night.

She is someone to hug gaining comfort from her very presence.

She is a helper, a friend, and a perfect joy to experience.

God's gift a privilege to watch her grow, develop, mature and succeed.

My sweetie kins, Tanya.

CUTIE

A single word—basic, unpretentious

Simple, short, sweet or complex, powerful and meaningful

I choose the latter.

An endearing name signifying someone special, precious, a treasured loved one.

Someone, who makes the room light up, puts a smile on your face, makes your chest burst with pride.

An all around nice person who has the gift of understanding, compassion and caring making the recipient feel happy, joyful and loved.

A person who understands without explanation.

Gives a hug instinctively, an all around good person.

Although far away, scholastically committed and earning his way, he remembers.

My cutie, my sweetie, my nephew, Nicholas.

Ba

His walk is tall, strong and sure

Arms folded stance determined

A man of purpose, principle and reason

Observing, watching, caring

Conflict, decisions, crisis his domain

Gentle persuasion, nudging, cajoling

His methods of choice

Offering comfort, sound advice, motivation, inspiration

All in the name of guidance and leadership for his family.

His voice a gentle whisper powerful, knowledgeable, wise

His persona kind, experienced, firm in command.

Always available, accountable, ready to give assistance

Listening, hearing, understanding without judgment or malice

No problem too large or too small

Distance, time and place no obstacle

Standing at your side, hand on your shoulder secure

A man of substance, character and courage

Honored, respected, cherished

Rock solid, dependable, steadfast

Title earned, valued, privileged

Father, friend, confidant

A special person, Ba.

PAM

Out in the country, Lancaster, PA

Farmland, pastures, hills and valleys

Amish farmers, animals and crops

Neighbors all welcomed with openness and respect

Plentiful bounty appreciated and enjoyed

Mooing, grunting, clucking, nature's alarm clock

A lovely house open, inviting, unpretentious

Husband Tom, friend and soul mate

The love and joy of her life.

A dog named Snugs at her side, a loyal companion

An email guru jokes, current information, facts and tales

Uplifting moods and spirits brightening our day

Challenges met without preamble, compunction or fanfare

Straightforward, to the point, direct

Truthful, diplomatic, honest

Considerate of feelings and emotions, everyone equal and special

Dependable, caring, understanding, patient

Constant, dedicated, accountable, never faltering

A trusted confidant, a friend forever

My friend, Pam.

Jo

A distance away, a hectic commute

A lifestyle diverse, noisy and fun

A bit naughty, but oh so nice

Glamorous yet fashionable, stylish and chic

A thinker, writer and visionary.

Motivated, always striving for fulfillment in her achievements and goals working at full throttle success determined.

Wife and mother strong and wise, she possesses the virtue of inner strength and calm in times of crisis and adversity.

Powerfully linked with spirits and spirituality, an intuitive gift an insight into things yet to come.

A strength of courage and survival experienced at the horrific tragedy at 911 dealing with emotions and feelings too intense and personal for us to imagine. Seeing first hand life's last breath at the sight.

An unbreakable bond with family and friends offering assistance ready at a moment's notice, a helping hand, a shoulder to cry on, and most importantly a caring and strength so intense its recipient feels charged and energized.

Meditation of thoughts deep and complex. Knowledge and understanding beyond her years too much for our senses to absorb.

A giver, nurturer, confidant and cousin/sister. A powerful ally, grounded and loyal, my cousin, Josephine.

GUIDO

A kindred spirit
A kind heart
A gentle soul
An inspired chef dedicated to his profession
The kitchen his domain.

Pots clanging, utensils singing
Steam rising filling the air
Aromas swirling tantalizing and mysterious
Each plate eye appealing, a work of art.

Appetites sparked, senses whirling
Offering unique pleasure and enjoyment
His talent gifted, personified without boundary
He found his niche and performed it well.

His customers, his audience privileged
Special participants in sharing his creative bounty.
Someone who touched our hearts
Fed our spirits with love and kindness
Taught us courage and gave us strength
Showing us not to give up, to fight the battle.

His presence with us temporary, too short in time
We thank you Lord for sending us Guido.
We return him to you with all our prayers and love.
Watch over him, love him, keep him close
His loss is felt from within our hearts
He will be truly missed
Your special, precious gift to us
My cousin, Guido.

MICHAEL

Mike, Michael, Miguel, Michlein

Spelling, pronunciation of no consequence

The name is the same.

Constantly energized, motivated, always active on the go, moving, shaking running here, there, everywhere.

Testing nature's force, challenging life's obstacles, competitive in group projects and activities.

A bright talented intelligent young man, an excellent student, a best friend.

A dedicated son, loving brother respectful of his elders especially his grandmother, uncles and aunts.

Always at the ready offering words of comfort and understanding to all who know him.

A gentle soul, a soft heart, a special unique spirit, a kind person.

It is with a sense of pride, happiness and joy I introduce my nephew, Michael.

BRIDGET

Her grandmother's namesake

Sassy, feisty and energetic

Pretty as a picture

Cute as a button

Naughty and nice

Fashionable and stylish

A beautiful soul, a loving heart

Intelligent, loyal and true

An honor student scholastically

A UPS employee dedicated to her job

Modest and shy she strives to succeed

Working hard earning her way

Wisdom, understanding and caring beyond her years

Fellow workers and friends singing her praise

Parents and family bursting with love and pride

Special and unique a no nonsense attitude

Strong and tall, poetry in motion

My niece, Bridget.

EPILOGUE

I have discovered that my profession, career and journey have been stepping stones to what I believe is success. I have been trying to do my best in my job and making myself more informed and knowledgeable. My experience has taught me that respect for myself as a human being and a spiritual person is more valuable than all the money, promotions and career moves I have ever obtained. My sense of respect for myself has honored me with the ultimate achievement of earning the respect, trust, concern and confidence from the people who are in my space. Nothing can be more precious than that. Title, fame and fortune are not worthwhile without respect. This knowledge I pass on to you. I know you will take it to heart and use it wisely. I have learned that this is the legacy I will leave behind.

Breinigsville, PA USA
06 November 2009
227160BV00002B/3/P